Praise for the Humorists' Guides

"A first-rate gift for the traveler-to-be as well as for stay-at-homes." —*New York Times*

"Whether you want help deciding what kind of cream soup the London sky resembles or just want to read a play-by-play analysis of Italy's national sport—*fare rumore* (making noise)—the Humorists' Guides will serve you well." —*Travel & Leisure*

"What better companion than classic travel humor. "
—*Washington Post*

"They're all great fun." —*Travel-Holiday*

"The perfect books to get the traveller in the proper mood for the vagaries of travel in unfamiliar surroundings." —*Toronto Globe and Mail*

"When you're tired of Frommer, Fielding and Fodor, here's where to turn." —*Columbus Dispatch*

Other Humorists' Guides

HERE WE ARE

• • • • • • • • • • •

THE HUMORISTS' GUIDE TO THE UNITED STATES

Edited by Robert Wechsler

CATBIRD PRESS

CATBIRD PRESS
44 North Sixth Avenue
Highland Park, NJ 08904
908-572-0816

Distributed to the trade by Independent Publishers Group

The Humorists' Guides are available at special bulk-purchase
discounts for promotions, premiums, and fund-raising.
For details, contact Catbird Press at the above address.

The publisher wishes to acknowledge permission to include
in this book copyright material as follows:

CHARLES ALLBRIGHT: Reprinted from *The Best of the Arkansas Traveler,* ed.
Maylon T. Rice, August House, by permission of the publisher.
Copyright 1986 Maylon T. Rice. ACKNOWLEDGMENTS are continued at
the back of the book.

Library of Congress Cataloging-in-Publication Data

Here we are: the humorists' guide to the United States
edited by Robert Wechsler
        p.   cm.
ISBN 0-945774-13-3 (pbk. : alk. paper) : $10.95
1. United States—Description and travel—Humor.
I. Wechsler, Robert, 1954-
E161.5.H47   1991
917.304'92—dc20   91-6687

CONTENTS

INTRODUCTION

THE UNITED STATES IS BIG. Yes, China, the Soviet Union, and Brazil are also big, but they don't send many tourists to America. To those who do come, the United States is big as they come. Its buildings are big, its roads are big, its stores and its malls are big, and for those who manage to get out of the tourist centers of the biggest cities, its hearts are big as well. But most of all, its distances are big. And then, of course, there's Texas.

Travel humor is a matter of points of view: funny, ironic, eccentric, surprising ways to look at places and people. It's scarcely one of the oldest professions, but there is a rich lode of writing by some of our greatest humorists and travel writers. Taken in sufficient doses, it is guaranteed to make you look differently at traveling and enjoy it more.

Travel humorists won't guide you through any museums or tell you where you can find the best bargains in hotels, jewelry, or souvenirs. They can't tell you which cities you absolutely must see if you have only seven days to cover the better part of a continent. But they *can* make you see a city or a river or a walk in the woods in a completely new light, and they can introduce you to people and places that are on nobody's itinerary.

Travel humor about the United States has an extra element of fun for us Americans, because it's *us* the writers are talking about rather than *them*. We're the natives and, in many cases, the tourists too. It's *our* customs and holidays and manners that are under examination, either by outright foreigners or by Americans from a different part of the land.

Before I write another word, I should state my prejudices or, at least, my origins. I am a native of Pittsburgh, Pennsylvania, and a resident of a small town in Central New Jersey, and I have lived roughly half my adult life in Boston and the other half in the New York City area (though only three years actually in the Big Apple). In other words, I'm a big-city Northeasterner with a touch of the Midwest who lives in a small town. You can take this for what it's worth.

The history of travel humor about America is a checkered one. Many of the early works go almost unrepresented here because they were so prejudiced and nasty, and dwelt so much on customs which, like the fine art of spitting, have long since been replaced by such customs as the fine art of graffiti. The first major humorous look at America, Frances Trollope's *Domestic Manners of the Americans* (1832), doesn't have a single passage that fits the spirit of this collection. And as much as I am a great fan of Charles Dickens, and have included selections from his works in three of my other *Humorists' Guides,* his *American Notes* (1842) is similarly outdated in its prejudices (but I have included an excerpt from one of his letters).

Anthony Trollope, the son of Frances, gave an accurate description of the travel humor of the first half of the nineteenth century in his own attempt to take on the Big Country, *North America* (1862): "The writings which have been most popular in England on the subject of the United States have hitherto dealt chiefly with social details; and though in most cases true and useful, have created laughter on one side of the Atlantic, and soreness on the other." Anthony Trollope also touched on the essence of travel humor: "The traveller who desires to tell his experience of North America must write of people rather than of things."

The British were certainly not the only ones to write travelogues of America in the nineteenth century; the French were equally fascinated with the Big Place across the Atlantic. But as with the British, most of their books were serious critiques of the American government, economy, and society. The first skilled foreign writer to come to America without attacking or admiring institutions from slavery to job mobility was, of all people, Rudyard Kipling, in 1889. Since then, it's been open country, and the British and French, Germans and Russians, Canadians and Mexicans have found something to laugh or at least smile about in their travels through America.

As for Americans, the father of travel humor, Mark Twain, wrote *Roughing It* in 1872, and many of the humorists of his generation, such as Bill Nye and Artemus Ward, used their speaking tours as a good occasion for adding a few choice words to the young art of travel humor.

Although during the classic years of written humor in America, the 1920s and 1930s, the emphasis was on humor about Europe, the great humorists of the time couldn't help poking a little fun at the absurdities of domestic travel. And both humorists and "serious" writers came from Europe to see the young nation in all its burgeoning silliness.

Once America grew to be Number One after the Second World War, it drew humorists, journalists, essayists, and all the other -ists like flypaper. Everyone here and abroad seemed to be hopping into a plane or a car to see the land of the supermarket and the atom bomb. And then, to recoup some of the travel expenses, they wrote about it in one of the seemingly infinite number of magazines and newspapers.

But, like everything else, traveling matured. People started traveling in much greater numbers and demanding information. And getting it, all sorts of it. Information happens to be the enemy of travel humor. You can impart information in a humorous way, but the journalist or travel guidist has to give at least the appearance of responsibility. And humor can't bear appearances, especially responsible ones. But somehow travel humor has survived the video age, especially humor about traveling in the United States.

I would like to thank all the people who have made this book possible. I would like to thank Larry Wallberg, who did a large part of the research for this book; Pat Lesnefsky, who typed a great pile of manuscript into the computer; Mircea Vasiliu, who somehow captured American travel humor in a single illustration on the cover; Leonard Ringel and Janet Parker, who designed the series cover and this specific cover, respectively; Axiom Design Systems in New York City, which set the type; New England Book Components, which printed the cover; and Arcata Graphics/Fairfield, which printed and bound the book. And finally, I want to thank the all-too-forgotten souls who work in the permissions departments of the authors' publishing houses, the authors' families, the authors' agents, and even the authors and artists themselves, who were kind enough to let me include their writing in this collection.

I would like to end my introduction with two excerpts from other people's introductions to books about traveling in America. More than anything I've read, British writer G. K. Chesterton's words sum up the philosophy of the *Humorists' Guides*. And Anthony Trollope's words sum up the problem of writing good but not overly offensive travel humor.

By the way, occasionally you will see a * * * in the middle of a selection. This means that some irrelevant text has been left out, either about something other than traveling through America or about something that means nothing today, or I've just decided to cut a selection down to an easily digestible size. Also, please note that nearly all of the selection titles are mine, not the authors'.

G.K. Chesterton
On Taking Amusement Seriously 1922

I HAVE NEVER MANAGED to lose my old conviction that travel narrows the mind. At least a man must make a double effort of moral humility and imaginative energy to prevent it from narrowing his mind. Indeed there is something touching and even tragic about the thought of the thoughtless tourist, who might have stayed at home loving Laplanders, embracing Chinamen, and clasping Patagonians to his heart in Hampstead or Surbiton, but for his blind and suicidal impulse to go and see what they looked like. This is not meant for nonsense; still less is it meant for the silliest sort of nonsense, which is cynicism. The human bond that he feels at home is not an illusion. On the contrary, it is rather an inner reality. Man is inside all men. In a real sense any man may be inside any men. But to travel is to leave the inside and draw dangerously near the outside. So long as he thought of men in the abstract, like naked toiling figures in some classic frieze, merely as those who labour and love their children and die, he was thinking the fundamental truth about them. By going to look at their unfamiliar manners and customs he is inviting them to disguise themselves in fantastic masks and costumes. Many modern internationalists talk as if men of different nationalities had only to meet and mix and understand each other. In reality that is the moment of supreme danger—the moment when they meet. We might shiver, as at the old euphemism by which a meeting meant a duel.

Travel ought to combine amusement with instruction; but most travellers are so much amused that they refuse to be instructed. I do not blame them for being amused; it is perfectly natural to be amused at a Dutchman for being Dutch or a Chinaman for being Chinese. Where they are wrong is that they take their own amusement seriously.

They base on it their serious ideas of international instruction. It was said that the Englishman takes his pleasures sadly; and the pleasure of despising foreigners is one which he takes most sadly of all. He comes to scoff and does not remain to pray, but rather to excommunicate. Hence in international relations there is far too little laughing, and far too much sneering. But I believe that there is a better way which largely consists of laughter; a form of friendship between nations which is actually founded on differences. To hint at some such better way is the only excuse of this book.

Anthony Trollope
A Favourable Verdict 1862

IF I COULD DO ANYTHING to mitigate the soreness, if I could in any small degree add to the good feeling which should exist between two nations which ought to love each other so well, and which do hang upon each other so constantly, I should think that I had cause to be proud of my work.

But it is very hard to write about any country a book that does not represent the country described in a more or less ridiculous point of view. It is hard at least to do so in such a book as I must write. A De Tocqueville may do it. It may be done by any philosophico-political or politico-statistical, or statistico-scientific writer; but it can hardly be done by a man who professes to use a light pen, and to manufacture his article for the use of general readers. Such a writer may tell all that he sees of the beautiful; but he must also tell, if not all that he sees of the ludicrous, at any rate the most piquant part of it. How to do this without being offensive is the problem which a man with such a task before him has to solve. His first duty is owed to his readers, and consists mainly in this: that he shall tell the truth, and shall so tell that truth that what he has written may be readable. But a second duty is due to those of whom he writes; and he does not perform that duty well if he gives offense to those, as to whom, on the summing up of the whole evidence for and against them in his own mind, he intends to give a favourable verdict. There are of course those against whom a writer does not intend to give a favourable verdict;—people and places whom he desires to describe on the peril of his own judgment, as bad, ill-educated, ugly, and odious. In such cases his course is straightforward enough. His judgment may be in great peril, but his volume or chapter will be easily written. Ridicule and censure run glibly from the pen, and form themselves into sharp paragraphs which are pleasant to the reader. Whereas eulogy is commonly dull, and too frequently sounds as though it were false. There is much difficulty in expressing a verdict which is intended to be favourable; but which, though favourable, shall not be falsely eulogistic; and though true, not offensive.

FELLOW CITIZENS

Observation Platform

✒Americans

✒*Americans are what America is all about, so why not start right off with the Uncle Sams, yankees, hillbillies, cowboys, Southern gentlepersons, and imperialist pigs that make America great, at least for travel humorists.*

With one exception, all the selections in this part of the book are by foreigners. After all, who can better describe our absurdities than people who don't live with them day in and day out, people who can compare our behavior to that of people elsewhere?

It's generally accepted that it's bad for a scientist to have too strong an effect on his experiments. However, this rule does not apply to travel humorists. Some of their best material comes from being the odd person out: a Briton in the midst of Revolutionary War propaganda, an Asian among people who cannot discriminate among Asians, or a European reading a newspaper closer in size to an encyclopedia than to the newspapers back home. Our foreigners look at the way we talk (and talk and talk), the way we celebrate our holidays and play our games and, most of all, the way we see ourselves and present ourselves to the outside world.

None of the authors in this section is a household name here, but they are all excellent travel writers with excellent senses of humor, lacking only excellent PR. The authors include British naval captain cum novelist Frederick Marryat, Philippine General Carlos P. Romulo, and the sole American travel writer, Julian Street, whose book Abroad at Home *could almost be considered a foreigner's view.*

Elijah Brown
All Talk 1913

THE AMERICAN is an incessant talker, he will talk about himself, his family, his business, his dollars, his religion, and his country, so unreservedly, that in half an hour's time you are made pretty well acquainted with all that there is worth knowing about him; you know his history from his cradle to the present moment; he is so expansive, that to a sympathetic listener he will talk about himself 'clear down to his boots,' as he would say, but unfortunately he expects you to do the same in return, and that is one reason why, at heart, he does not really love an Englishman.

The American carries his nature on the surface and keeps little hidden by way of reserve.

You may go into his office and find him entirely immersed in work, so busy with it, he will tell you, that he has scarcely time to sneeze, yet that same man will waste a solid hour talking to you about it.

Thérèse Yelverton
Delicacy and the American Woman 1875

AN AMERICAN WOMAN is deficient both in external as well as internal delicacy. Her bosom knows no sacred privacy. She will start and tell you her whole family history and affairs before you have known her half an hour. A lady—*of fashion,* at all events—after an introduction on a steamer, told me the whole history of her life; the disagreeable character of her two husbands, the latter of whom had recklessly squandered the handsome property the first had left her, and of which she ought to have had the full enjoyment, as she certainly married him for it, and he died two years after, being much older than her own father. We suggested that it would probably have been as well to have remained a widow. She appeared to take a retrospective glance, then replied, she "felt lonesome," she "felt like marrying again."

One lady told me on making her return-call, of a piece of scandal that had been afloat concerning herself some years before, and which most women would have preferred to have kept to themselves. A second, on her first visit, entertained me with the details of a horrible surgical operation she had gone through. Another with the cruelty and infidelity of her husband. This lady, commenting on the interview to another, a mutual friend, exclaimed, "What a provoking creature that Mrs. —— is, she never said a word about herself."

C.V.R. Thompson
Three Americans 1939

THERE WERE THREE AMERICANS at my table. I felt like a block of ice in the middle of three camp fires. They were so friendly I thought they had been brought up together, but they had never met until ten minutes before.

I had not met many Americans, but I had a very definite picture of my typical American.

His face was long and lean. His cheeks were creased like the skin of a rather green baked apple. His arms and legs were thick and muscular from playing golf before breakfast, after luncheon, and during most of dinner. His body was upright, but a little paunchy from worrying about the good things he couldn't eat. His eyes, not necessarily obscured by the traditional horn-rimmed spectacles, squinted from watching if the fellow next to him was getting a little further ahead than he. His hair was a theatrical gray, because he was flattered to think other people were thinking he was prematurely gray.

He talked rapidly with the voice of a radio announcer chewing sandpaper. He seldom argued, and he never listened. He had never heard of Constable or Tennyson. But he was an authority on Rembrandts because they cost a million dollars, on Bernard Shaw because he knew more about ballyhoo than any American, on Whistler because his portrait of his mother was used for a postage stamp.

He preferred blondes, particularly when tired. He never had his nails manicured without making an assignation with the manicurist. He had a plump and opulent wife.

He was something in Wall Street, something in Chicago, or just something in pork. The dollar was his god. It would bring Buckingham Palace brick by brick to Zilmerville, Wisconsin. It would buy him anything from a pound of imported cheese to a free pardon for committing murder. Women or horses. Apartments or continents.

A costly suit was necessarily a good suit, even if it was a vulgar check—which it usually was. An expensive movie was essentially a great movie. And an extravagant wife was necessarily the best little wife in all Wisconsin.

He was always beating the big drum. His hometown might be a fleck on the map, but it was *the* most thriving, *the* most progressive, *the* most stupendous little town in the world. By the same token, America was God's own country. It ruled the world. Of course, it won the War, but it also won the peace. "Why, we in America wouldn't stand for conditions like these in England," he would say. "There are 2,341 millionaires in America. America is the land of opportunity, the land of progress, the land of wealth. Why, the gold in America stretched end to end would. . ."

Always the Dollar, the most-used word in the American language, the Almighty God, Dollar.

In other words, my typical American was, to borrow his own vernacular, a pretty average pain in the neck.

I was delighted with the Californian at my table. He seemed to match so perfectly the subject of my preconceived portrait. The only difference was that where my

Average American would use the word dollar, my Californian used the word California.

But his face was long and lean, his cheeks creased. He talked all through one course about his game of golf at St. Andrew's. He pecked at his food, and I had the definite impression he would have preferred a tin of sodium bicarbonate. He bragged about his home state. "There's no place like it in the world. Paradise on earth. Once you've been there you never want to leave." But I found that it wasn't business that had kept him on the French Riviera all winter.

He was apparently something in wheat. He bragged about all the wheat he had, about the millions he would have made if the Depression had not brought down the price of wheat. Over coffee he announced that America had won the War, that there never would have been any war if England had not come in too late. He squelched my one attempt to enter the conversation by his obvious compassion for me because I was making my first transatlantic crossing.

After dinner I saw him with the only blonde on board, and I learned later that he made a great impression on her because he pretended he was one of the survivors of the *Titanic* disaster.

Just as I had decided that my opinions of Americans were painfully accurate, my decisions were completely upset by the other two Americans at the table.

They had at first seemed so friendly with the Californian that I had automatically classed them with him. But on the second day out, one of them, short and dark, with what the advertisements call a perpetual five o'clock shadow, turned on the Californian during one of his interminable lectures on the beauties of his home state. He was quite insulting, but I didn't find out how insulting until a long time after. I didn't know then that the worst thing you can say to a Californian is to tell him how much you like Florida.

Grateful to my neighbor, I studied him more closely, and I found that he did not fit into my picture at all. He was a traveling salesman—in steel rails, I believe. He did not play golf. In fact, he didn't give a hang for athletics of any kind. He didn't boast about his home town; I actually had to ask him before I discovered he was a New Yorker. He didn't talk unless he had something to say—and that was usually interesting. He knew a great deal more about the European situation than I did. And he didn't seem to care much whether American had won the War or not.

He ate heartily of what he wanted without doing any mental arithmetic about the calories in the dishes he ordered. He was kindly and helpful. He whispered a warning to me when in a spirit of ignorant adventure I ordered from the American menu two strangely named dishes, each of which was a meal in itself. In only one respect did he conform with my idea of an American. When he ordered oysters—which was at nearly every meal—he always asked for "ersters."

The third American was different again. In spite of his blue evening clothes and his baldish head, he looked more like a figure out of a Dutch Old Master than an American. Perhaps that was because he really was a Dutchman. He called himself an American, of course, and he *was* an American citizen, but a century back his ancestors had tended a windmill in Holland. "But that was a century ago," he said, rather testily, when I explained that I would consider him a Dutchman, "and my folks have lived in Philadelphia for three generations." A little exasperated at his stubbornness, I tried to make him see that a century is only a hundred years. But he wouldn't listen. To him—as to nearly all Americans, it seems—a century is a whole era in the world's history.

Margaret Powell
Bloody Brits! 1973

IT WAS SOMEWHAT EMBARRASSING for me when we came to the oil-painting representing the 'Declaration of Independence'. 'See that?' said this noisy American. 'That means something, that does. That's when we kicked out the bloody British. We showed them they couldn't run our country. Lot of lousy imperialists they were. As for their king he was as mad as a hatter.'

I kept very quiet while all this ranting was going on. I had no desire to remind him that I was British. Perhaps I ought to have felt patriotic enough to protest at this slight to our royalty. But as I didn't know George III personally, I couldn't see that it was my duty to point out that he wasn't mad all the time; that somebody has discovered he was suffering from porphyria—something to do with the metabolism. However, without consulting me, my large friend nudged the American and said, 'This lady is British.' I could have sunk through the floor. Nevertheless, I thought that the American might have apologized to me for his anti-British remarks. But far from it—all he said was, 'Well, ma'am, we beat you in one war, and helped you to win the last two.' Insufferable man! I suppose, being a stranger in his country, I should not have answered, 'You were a bit late in helping us win the first one.' But I was really irritated by then at his chauvinistic attitude: after all, he wasn't even there. I expected him to be furious at my remark, but surprisingly he burst out laughing, 'Ma'am, you had me there.'

Julian Street
What's the Matter. . . 1914

IF YOU ASK A BUFFALO MAN what is the matter with his city, he will, very likely, sit down with great solemnity and try to tell you, and even call a friend to help him, so as to be sure that nothing is overlooked. He may tell you that the city lacks one great big dominating man to lead it into action; or that there has been, until recently, lack of cooperation between the banks; or that there are ninety or a hundred thousand Poles in the city and only about the same number of people springing from what may be called "old American stock." Or he may tell you something else.

If, upon the other hand, you ask a Minneapolis man that question, what will he do? He will look at you pityingly and think you are demented. Then he will tell you very positively that there is nothing the matter with Minneapolis, but that there is something definitely the matter with any one who thinks there is! Yes, indeed! If you want to find out what is the matter with Minneapolis, it is still necessary to go for information to St. Paul. As you proceed westward, such a question becomes increasingly dangerous.

Ask a Kansas City man what is wrong with his town and he will probably attack you; and as for Los Angeles—! Such a question in Los Angeles would mean the calling out of the National Guard, the Chamber of Commerce, the Rotary Club, and all the "boosters" (which is to say the entire population of the city); the declaring of martial law, a trial by summary courtmartial, and your immediate execution. The manner of your execution would depend upon the phrasing of your question. If you had asked: "Is there anything wrong with Los Angeles?" they'd probably be content with selling you a city lot and then hanging you; but if you said: "What is wrong with Los Angeles?" they would burn you at the stake and pickle your remains in vitriol.

George Mikes
Comics and the Rest 1948

I ALWAYS FELT SLIGHTLY INSULTED when I bought a
newspaper in America. For three or four cents the newsvendor handed over a bulky volume of about eighty pages
and I hadn't the slightest hope of reading more of it than the
headlines and a few paragraphs here and there. What would
you feel if on entering a restaurant and ordering roast beef,
the waiters were to bring you three whole oxen with half a
ton of Idaho potatoes (an Idaho potato is as large as a
sizable marrow), or if you asked for a Frankfurter and six
waiters dragged up a fourteen-yard long pole of meat and
placed an ancient yataghan and a pitchfork beside your
plate? I always felt just as you would feel in such a case
whenever I received the usual overdose of my morning
paper. I had to read it in a hurry, almost in a panic, because
the evening papers are published early and if one loses any
precious time, one can never catch up with it again. A friend
of mine, a visitor from Tahiti, once remarked to me:

'In a month's time I'll go back to Tahiti. There, you know,
we have a two-page news sheet published daily. It gives
only the gist of world events and each item consists of two
or three lines. No baseball, no sensational licence cases, no
boxing matches, no murder stories and no twelve column
reports on unimportant speeches by unimportant politicians. Just the gist of the news, fairly balanced and written
in a rather dull manner, with the aloofness of a detached
observer. I'll go back to Tahiti and there I shall know once
again what is happening in New York.'

As far as I could make out, in America nobody reads
political news in any case. Women read the advertisements
only; schoolchildren the comic strips, also called—for some
unknown reason—the 'funnies'; well-dressed people read
the sports news and people in rags read only the stock

exchange report. (Or, may be, *vice versa:* people who read the stock exchange reports only, are always clad in rags.)

A humorists' look at Americans cannot be complete without a look at our fun and games. Fun in the form of our most boisterous national holiday—the Fourth of July—and our most boisterous national sports—football and politics. All of them viewed by British travel writers.

Capt. Frederick Marryat
The Fourth 1839

THE 4TH OF JULY, the sixty-first anniversary of American independence!

Pop—pop—bang—pop—pop—bang—bang—bang! Mercy on us! how fortunate it is that anniversaries come only once a year. Well, the Americans may have great reason to be proud of this day, and of the deeds of their forefathers, but why do they get so confoundedly drunk? why, on this day of independence, should they become so *dependent* upon posts and rails for support?—The day is at last over; my head aches, but there will be many more aching heads to-morrow morning!

What a combination of vowels and consonants have been put together! what strings of tropes, metaphors, and allegories, have been used on this day! what varieties and gradations of eloquence! There are at least fifty thousand cities, town, villages, and hamlets, spread over the surface of America—in each the Declaration of Independence has been read; in all one, and in some two or three, orations have been delivered, with as much gunpowder in them as in the squibs and crackers. But let me describe what I actually saw.

The commemoration commenced, if the day did not, on the evening of the 3d, by the municipal police going round and pasting up placards, informing the citizens of New York, that all persons letting off fireworks would be taken into custody, which notice was immediately followed up by the little boys proving their independence of the authorities, by letting off squibs, crackers, and bombs; and cannons, made out of shinbones, which flew in the face of every passenger, in the exact ratio that the little boys flew in the face of the authorities. This continued the whole night, and thus was ushered in the great and glorious day, illumined by a bright and glaring sun (as if bespoken on purpose by the mayor and corporation), with the thermometer at 90° in the shade. The first sight which met the eye after sunrise, was the precipitate escape, from a city visited with the plague of gunpowder, of respectable or timorous people in coaches, carriages, waggons, and every variety of vehicle. "My kingdom for a horse!" was the general cry of all those who could not stand fire. In the mean while, the whole atmosphere was filled with independence. Such was the quantity of American flags which were hoisted on board of the vessels, hung out of windows, or carried about by little boys, that you saw more stars at noon-day than ever could be counted on the brightest night. . . . Martial music sounded from a dozen quarters at once; and as you turned your head, you tacked to the first bars of a march from one band, the concluding bars of Yankee Doodle from another. At last the troops of militia and volunteers, who had been gathering in the park and other squares, made their appearance, well dressed and well equipped, and, in honour of the day, marching as independently as they well could. I did not see them go through many manoeuvres, but there was one which they appeared to excel in, and that was grounding arms and eating pies. * * *

Then the troops marched up into town again, and so did I follow them as I used to do the reviews in England, when a boy. All creation appeared to be independent on this day; some of the horses particularly so, for they would not keep "in no line not no how." Some preferred going sideways like crabs, others went backwards, some would not go at all, others went a great deal too fast, and not a few parted company with their riders, whom they kicked off just to shew their independence; but let them go which way they would, they could not avoid the squibs and crackers. And the women were in the same predicament: they might dance right, or dance left, it was only out of the frying-pan into the fire, for it was pop, pop; bang, bang; fiz, pop, bang, so that you literally trod upon gunpowder.

When the troops marched up Broadway, louder even than the music were to be heard the screams of delight from the children at the crowded windows on each side. "Ma! ma! there's pa!" "Oh! there's John." "Look at uncle on his big horse."

The troops did not march in very good order, because, independently of their not knowing how, there was a great deal of independence to contend with. At one time an omnibus and four would drive in and cut off the general and his staff from his division; at another, a cart would roll in and insist upon following close upon the band of music; so that it was a mixed procession—Generals, omnibus and four, music, cartloads of bricks, troops, omnibus and pair, artillery, hackney-coach, &c. &c. Notwithstanding all this, they at last arrived at the City Hall, when those who were old enough heard the Declaration of Independence read for the sixty-first time; and then it was—"Begone, brave army, and don't kick up a row." * * *

Unless you are an amateur, there is no occasion to go to the various places of public amusement where the fireworks are let off, for they are sent up every where in such quantities that you hardly know which way to turn your eyes. It is, however, adviseable to go into some place of safety, for the little boys and the big boys have all got their supply of rockets, which they fire off in the streets—some running horizontally up the pavement, and sticking into the back of a passenger; and others mounting slantingdicularly and Paul-Prying into the bed-room windows on the third floor or attics, just to see how things are going on *there*. Look in any point of the compass, and you will see a shower of rockets in the sky: turn from New York to Jersey City, from Jersey City to Brooklyn, and shower is answered by shower on either side of the water. Hoboken repeats the signal: and thus it is carried on to the east, the west, the north, and the south, from Rhode Island to the Missouri, from the Canada frontier to the Gulf of Mexico. At the various gardens the combinations were very beautiful, and exceeded anything that I had witnessed in London or Paris . . . all America was in a blaze; and, in addition to this mode of manifesting its joy, all America was tipsy.

There is something grand in the idea of national intoxication. In this world, vices on a grand scale dilate into virtues; he who murders one man, is strung up with ignominy; but he who murders twenty thousand has a statue to his memory, and is handed down to posterity as a hero. A staggering individual is a laughable and, sometimes, a disgusting spectacle; but the whole of a vast continent reeling, offering a holocaust of its brains for mercies vouchsafed, is an appropriate tribute of gratitude for the rights of equality and the *levelling spirit* of their institutions.

E. M. Delafield
My First Game of Football   1934

NOVEMBER 18th.—Go to see football game, Harvard *v.* Army. Am given to understand—and can readily believe—that this is a privilege for which Presidents, Crowned Heads, and Archbishops would one and all give ten years of life at the very least. It has only been obtained for me by the very greatest exertions on the part of everybody.

Fanny says that I shall be frozen—(can well believe it)—but that it will be worth it, and Leslie thinks I may find it rather difficult to follow—but it will be worth it—and they both agree that there is always a risk of pneumonia in this kind of weather. Wonder if they are going to add that it will still be worth it, because if so, shall disagree with them forcibly—but they heap coals of fire on my head for this unworthy thought by offering to lend me rugs, furs, muf- flers, and overshoes. Escort has been provided to me in the person of an admirer of Fanny's—name unknown to me from first to last—and we set out together at one o'clock. Harvard stadium is enormous—no roof, which I think a mistake—and we sit in open air, and might be comfortable if temperature would only rise above zero. Fanny's admirer is extremely kind to me, and can only hope he isn't thinking all the time how much pleasanter it would be if he were only escorting Fanny instead.

(Reminiscence here of once-popular song: "I am dancing with tears in my eyes, 'Cos the girl in my arms isn't you." Have always felt this attitude rather hard on girl actually being danced with at the moment of singing.)

Ask questions that I hope sound fairly intelligent, and listen attentively to the answers. Escort in return then paralyses me by putting to me various technical points in regard to what he calls the English Game. Try frantically to recall everything that I can ever remember having heard from Robin, but am only able to recollect that he once said Soccer was absolutely lousy and that I rebuked him for it. Translate this painful reminiscence into civilised version to the effect that Rugger is more popular than Soccer with our Schoolboys.

Presently a mule appears and is ridden round the field by a member of one team or the other—am not sure which— and I observe, idiotically, that It's like a Rodeo—and imme- diately perceive that it isn't in the least, and wish I hadn't spoken. Fortunately a number of young gentlemen in white suddenly emerge on to the ground, turn beautiful back somersaults in perfect unison, and cheer madly through a megaphone. Am deeply impressed, and assure Fanny's admirer that we have nothing in the least like that at

Wembley, Twickenham, nor, so far as I know, anywhere else. He agrees, very solemnly, that the cheers are a Great Feature of the Game.

Soon afterwards we really get started, and I watch my first game of American football. Players all extensively padded and vast numbers of substitute-players wait about in order to rush in and replace them when necessary. Altogether phenomenal number of these exchanges takes place, but as no stretchers visible, conclude that most of the injuries received fall short of being mortal.

Fanny's admirer gives me explanations about what is taking place from time to time, but is apt to break off in the middle of a phrase when excitement overcomes him. Other interruptions are occasioned by organised yellings and roarings, conducted from the field, in which the spectators join.

At about four o'clock it is said to be obvious that Harvard hasn't got a chance, and soon afterwards the Army is declared to have won.

Escort and I look at each other and say Well, and Wasn't it marvellous, and then stand up and I discover that I am quite unable to feel my feet at all, and that all circulation in the rest of my body has apparently stopped altogether— probably frozen.

We totter as best we can through the crowd—escort evidently just as cold as I am, judging by the color of his face and hands—and over bridge, past buildings that I am told are all part of the College, and to flat with attractive view across the river. As I have not been warned by anybody that this is in store, I remain unaware throughout why I am being entertained there, or by whom. Hot tea, for once, is extraordinarily welcome, and so is superb log-fire; and I talk to unknown, but agreeable, American about President Roosevelt, the state of the dollar—we both take a gloomy view of this—and extreme beauty of American foliage in the woods of Maine—where I have never set foot, but about which I have heard a good deal.

A. G. MacDonnell
The American Fantasy 1935

THE HUGE AIRPORT AT DALLAS was crowded with aeroplanes. In the hangars there were swarms of little biplanes, some painted black and yellow in stripes, like wasps, and some bright scarlet so that they looked like Richthofen's squadron, but on the field itself there were rows of great silver monoplanes, Douglas and Boeing machines, roaring away as their engines were being warmed up for action. They were all private machines, belonging to oil-magnates who were holding a Conference that very morning in Dallas, and they were a great deal more beautiful than their owners, whom I saw later on at luncheon in the hotel.

That luncheon, attended by hundreds of oil-magnates with their attendant sub-magnates, secretaries, advisers, and politicians, put the last nail into the coffin of Texas. Gone forever is my boyhood vision. The derrick has taken the place of the bronco-buster, the legal injunction the place of the six-shooter, and the pasty, flabby-jowled expanse of slab-like countenance of the oil-magnate reigns where once were only lean and sun-tanned faces, blue-eyed, stern, yet with a ready smile.

Yet even in that exhibition of human codfish lurked something of the American fantasy. That is one of the never-ending charms of the place. You never know when something utterly absurd may not follow instantly on something utterly magnificent, and vice versa. Round every corner there may be a Wonder of the World, or a crime, or a rather bad joke, or an ideal, or a dump of rusty cans. You cannot tell which it is going to be. Of only one thing can you be certain, that round every corner you will find something. There is no such thing in America as a complete blank, except perhaps in women's clubs.

Consider the aspect of the American fantasy. . . . In California the name of the gentleman who had guaranteed to produce Utopia out of a ballot-box, provided that it was sufficiently full of pro-Utopian votes, had been blazoned on billboards, splashed in newspaper advertisements, placarded on handbills all over the State. In California you could hardly walk fifty yards without seeing his name.

With only the brief interval of that day's transit across Arizona, I had now come to a State where a name was also blazoned on billboards, splashed in newspaper advertisements, placarded on handbills all over the State. In Texas you could hardly walk fifty yards without seeing the name. The name on the Californian billboards stood for the downfall of the Capitalist system. The name on the Texan billboards stood for the triumph of the Capitalist system. The one represented the assault on vested interests, the other represented the apotheosis of vested interests. The one was the spearhead of the attack on Rugged Individualism, the other a shield for the defence. The one cried, "Share the wealth"; the other cried, "Give me the wealth." The one cried, "Give me the power and I'll give you Utopia"; the other thought, "I have the power and so I have Utopia." And the names were the same.

ፙBecause, at least so far, nearly all published travel humorists have been white, the large black and Asian populations in America have been largely ignored or viewed as little more than a curiosity. In the following selections, Philippine General Romulo is the subject of a bet about national origin, and British writer J. B. Priestley turns an ironic eye on American race relations.

Brig. Gen. Carlos P. Romulo
A Bet 1945

IN ONE RAILWAY STATION RESTAURANT four soldiers were arguing and pointing at me, until I coaxed the waitress into telling me what the argument was about.

"They can't decide whether you are Chinese or Hawaiian," she answered reluctantly.

After finishing my meal I went over and joined them. "All right, fellows, how much money is up?"

There were four one-dollar bills on the table.

"Two of us have bet you are Chinese and two that you are Hawaiian," one of the soldiers said.

"You're all wrong," I answered. "I'm a Filipino. So, pay me."

They laughed and pushed over the bills. I took them. I had to.

"Perhaps this will cover the price of five drinks," I suggested.

There were two merry rounds before I had to dash for my train.

J. B. Priestley
Our Sense of Superiority 1955

THE VOICES I HEARD in the dining-car belonged to the South-West. The men's were deep, almost cavernous; the women's were higher than they are in the East, higher and more nasal, as if the summer dust compelled them to keep nose, throat, mouth, as little open as possible. The men, all middle-aged, were booming routine little jokes at one another, in a dutiful fashion, like hard-working character actors. While I waited for coffee and eggs there passed through the car, in the dark-blue uniform of the train staff, a solemn ebony giant, like some prince of the Niger. Now and again one sees a similar princely figure among the coloured dining-car waiters, as if some imperial family of the jungle had taken to serving orange juice and coffee; but these are infrequent. The majority always seems to me to divide itself into three strongly-marked types: oldish melancholy negroes, bent and furrowed with years of servility, later versions of poor Uncle Tom; then mischievous comedian types, who arrive and depart all one wide grin and can be overheard roaring with laughter just outside the car; and finally, certain paler, spectacled, younger men, efficient but almost haughtily withdrawn, who look as if they are taking your order for Navy Bean soup and pot roast only until they can complete their courses in sociology somewhere at the end of the line. And we diners might remember that between these sociologists, whose spectacles will coldly magnify our bad habits, and the comedians so apt at mimicry, and the diminishing glances of the giant black princes in disguise, not much of us will be left to bolster up our sense of superiority.

One of the hardest things for foreigners to understand about America is that there are large pockets of Americans who don't live like the world's view of Americans at all. There are Chinatowns and Little Italys, and Little Cubas, Little Lebanons, and Little Vietnams as well. In the last selection on Americans, British travel writer Cecil Roberts takes a journey from Chicago to New York, via Poland.

Cecil Roberts
A Journey Through Poland 1947

ONE NIGHT in Chicago's Loop district, in search of local colour, I went into an automat restaurant where, inserting nickels and dimes, one drew food out of specimen compartments. I sat at a table with a young giant, a lad of Polish-Lithuanian stock, born in America. He spoke English with a strong accent. Blue-eyed, blond, massive, he was a truck driver for a Chicago manufacturer whose products he delivered all over the country. He was greatly interested in my accent, nationality, profession, with a childlike curiosity. When we had eaten he invited me to a bowling alley in the next street, where we played. He consumed innumerable Coca-Colas, which he tried to induce me to drink, but I struck after the third. When I told him I was leaving soon for New York but was held up for want of a berth on the train he had a solution at once. "Hey now," he said, the preface to every sentence, "you come with me. I'll drive you there. I'm going to New York."

It would take five days, he said. He would show me the country. Realising I should see the country as I would never see it again, I overcame my hesitation and accepted. "Hey now!" he cried, jubilantly, giving me a slap on the back with a great hand that knocked the breath out of me. I asked when he was leaving. "Tomorrow night at ten," he said. "We go to Grand Rapids first, then Detroit." I hesitated; all-night driving was not my idea of travel. "Hey now, you'll be all right," he cried. He asked me where I was staying and said he would call for me.

The idea of setting forth from a fashionable hotel in a truck touched my sense of the ridiculous. It stunned the bellboy who brought down my portmanteau and watched me climb into a vehicle rimmed with rear lights. I sat in the high front of the van which then threaded its way out of the city. Two nights before I had driven through it on my way from the theatre in a large chauffeured limousine, between my host and hostess. In an adventurous life this would not be the least adventure.

But towards midnight I began to repent. It was a bitterly cold March night with snow shining on the flat countryside. My companion, George, saw I was shivering. "Hey now, Kyril!" he said, pulling up. He could not pronounce Cecil, and for the next four days I was Kyril. He got down, pulled off his greatcoat and insisted on my putting it over my own. He gave me his heavy leather driving gloves, and wrapped a rug around my knees, tucking me up as gently as a baby in a perambulator. He had nothing on but a heavy flannel lumberjack's shirt, with black and red squares, open at the throat. I protested that he would be cold. "Me cold!" he exclaimed, thumping his great chest, as though he were Tarzan about to bellow and leap.

We started off again, and above the roar of our truck he began to question me. He was very concerned about the blitzing of London. "Sure now that's wicked!" he kept saying. "And they knock down the churches, hey?" Little by little I learned his own story. His father came from near Cracow, his mother from Memel. There were nine children. They lived in four rooms and worked in the stockyards. "Not me—I live out, and I get out—isn't this better?" I agreed that it was. He was twenty-two, not married. "But I like dames. Some day I'll have kids. But I want 'em learned." "Learned?" I queried. He grinned at me with healthy animal teeth. "Yes, you're learned. I like to hear you talk. I always wanted education, but I was too dumb. Hey, but I'm not worrying. 'Still to ourselves in every place consigned, our own felicity we make or find,' " he repeated, with staccato syllables, adding, "Goldschmidt."

In the next four days I was to hear a stream of quotations, and I found the source when, among a pile of delivery invoices, a ragged little book fell out of his hand one morning. It was entitled *A Thought a Day* and was filled with quotations of the uplift variety. * * *

At seven o'clock we drew into Grand Rapids where George had three deliveries. Then we breakfasted in a corner drugstore with two policemen, and a cinema attendant who had been billsticking. George talked Polish with the bar attendant. In the talk I recognised only the name Annie. "That's a dame I knew. She's married a Marine. Hey, what-do-you-know! They get picked up these days. That's the third I've lost on this route," commented George. Half an hour later we were bound for Detroit, still in Michigan, which we reached after noon. There were more deliveries, then the truck was left in a yard. We lunched in a smelly little hothouse. I could hardly keep my eyes open. After lunch we went across to a barber's shop, but not in it. There was a narrow stairway with the legend, "Hotel Beds 75¢." To my amazement it was kept by another Pole.

We were shown a shabby room with two beds. George drew the blinds but it was still light. He took off all his clothes, and lit a cigarette. It was odd to see naked Hercules smoking. He watched me getting into my silk pajamas. "What's this!" he cried, derisively, picking up my jacket. "Hey now, only dames wear silk!" He roared with laughter. Then he opened a Coca-Cola bottle, and filled a glass. "Hey now, watch!" He stretched his body on the floor, placing the glass just above his head. Then to my amazement, with the greatest ease, he raised his legs over his head, took the glass between his feet, lifted it and, swinging his legs gently down again, deposited it on the floor. Then bending upwards, he leaned forward until his mouth touched the glass between his feet. Seizing it with his teeth, he raised it slowly, drank its contents, and then, arching backwards in a sudden spring, he deposited the glass on the floor under his body. With another spring he stood up, grinning triumphantly. The suppleness of that great body was amazing. He revelled in my astonishment. "Hey now, I ought to be in a circus!" he exclaimed, exultingly, getting into bed. * * *

We were in Cleveland at dawn. Here we made four deliveries and pushed on to Youngstown. This time after breakfast and delivery we went to a house in a dreary street, but our welcome was warm. It was a Polish household, relations of George's father. There was a pretty daughter who obviously was in love with George. He treated her cavalierly. "She's a soft egg," was his comment. I asked if he liked them "hard-boiled." "Hey, no, but I don't want 'em clammy." Poor girl, she sat and watched him eat as if Apollo had come to earth. I again contemplated the capricious cruelty of Eros. The next night at a dance hall in Scranton, George's partner, another Polish girl of no exterior attraction, was cruel in turn. George could not keep his hot hands off her. He gazed at her with the docile yearning of a spaniel and was snubbed unmercifully. "Hey, dames are hell!" he commented, despairingly.

I never found out who was who in that Polish warren at Youngstown. There were numerous children, a grandmother, a blind aunt, two daughters and four or five youths. Father I never saw; he cooked in a restaurant. The whole household talked Polish. George was a great favourite and he always seemed festooned with five of the grandchildren, to whom he gave "quarters." There was plenty of money in the house. Youngstown, like Cleveland and Detroit, was reeling with prosperity from war contracts, although then, March 1941, American was not in the war, but the great steel works were flaring night and day. * * *

We came into Pittsburgh by 2 A.M., the sky often lit by furnaces and smouldering slag heaps. The road in seemed interminable. I had often spoken in the city and been most generously entertained by its prominent citizens. Now I entered it, incognito, in a truck! After several deliveries we stopped about 2 A.M. at a roadhouse on the way out to Harrisburg. It was crammed even at this hour. Beyond the bar-restaurant we went down a passage to a large back room in which quite a hundred people were dancing to a jazz band. Drinks were being served all the time and George told me that many of the men went straight from the roadhouse to their work. Some were drunk but not incapably so. There was again a small Polish contingent in which I found myself. A very fat young woman seized me and insisted on dancing. I could not understand a single word she said. She reeked of beer and hamburgers. George took a malicious delight in my obvious discomfort. After twenty minutes in this little hell we got out into the cool night air. George saw I had hated the place, and was very apologetic. "Hey now, I thought you'd like to see it. I could show you a dozen joints like that." "One's enough," I answered. "I wonder the police don't close it." "Oh, they keep raiding it but it goes on. It's been closed down twice but it always opens up again. Two years ago it was only a shack. Now it's a gold mine."

We drove all night over the Allegheny Mountains to Harrisburg. It was a long drive, and bitterly cold. We were often at a height of two thousand feet. We made two halts at roadhouses where George was hailed as an old friend by the owners. At 10 A.M. we drew into Harrisburg. George had two deliveries here, but he wished to push on to Scranton where there was to be a Polish festival dance. It was another three or four hours' drive, and we should not get there until two or three o'clock in the afternoon. He suggested I should get into the van and sleep while he drove, but I was wide awake in the cold mountain air. * * *

Before we left Harrisburg, George gave me a surprise. "I'll show you St. Peter's, Rome, but the Pope doesn't live there, yet," he said, half playfully, half solemnly. I could not think what he meant until the truck suddenly ran into full view of the Capitol. It was a handsome building, and I saw at once what he meant. There, crowning it, was an excellent copy of the most famous dome in the world. * * *

I was not destined to see much of Scranton by day, for after two deliveries, and a quick meal at a snack-counter, George took me to our sleeping-quarters. Again they were in a private house, not relatives this time, but the occupants were Poles. We had a bedroom whose walls were decorated with what were presumably Polish religious texts. There was a chipped china Madonna and Bambino on a shelf, and some coloured wax effigies of emaciated saints with tin aureoles, pathetic expressions of peasant piety. We were soon fast asleep. We were to arise at 9 P.M. There was a Polish festival costume dance to which we were going, taking with us, according to George, "two of the loveliest girls you ever saw." I was utterly exhausted and would have foregone Helen of Troy herself for an extra hour in bed, but at half past eight George rudely woke me. * * *

Rosy as an apple, George opened the bag he had brought in from the truck. I watched him with eyes agog as he began to dress. He pulled on bright blue riding breeches with a yellow seam stripe, then a pale cream silk shirt embroidered at the neck band and at each wrist and over the twin breast pockets. I admired the flower embroidery in blue, red and gold silks. "My mother did it," he said proudly. Then he pulled on some high leather black boots, and wound round his waist a magenta cummerbund. Finally he stuck on his head a red cap with a blue peak, and a yellow flower embroidered on the crown. He looked magnificent, a giant who might have been a king's bodyguard. His hair was golden under the red cap, and his eyes, bright with excitement, were as blue as his breeches. He made a jump and a turn, slapping his boots, and came down with a bang that shook the building. "Hey now, what do you know!" he cried with a boyish grin. I felt like a shabby sparrow beside this cardinal bird. "But you're different," he said, consoling me. I was very much aware of it. "Now we'll go and collect them," he said. "You don't want a hat. C'm on!"

"Collect who—where?" I asked, bewildered, as he pushed me to the door.

"Dames! Boy, you wait," he cried jubilantly.

To my amazement we went upstairs, and with scarcely a pause into a room at the end of the landing. It was crammed with people and blazing with light. There were eight girls and four young men, with three old women and a very stout man. All the young people, girls and men, were dressed in gorgeous costumes. They were all laughing and shouting and putting the finishing touches to their attire. I was introduced to the old man and the three old ladies. Obviously George knew them all. To my dismay the whole company was talking Polish. I could not imagine how they could dance in this room, but a youth with silver hair, and long limbs clad in white skin-tight kid breeches and Cossack

41

boots, told me the dance was at a hall in the town. Two of the youths wore frogged dragoon coats, one sleeve loose. Most of the girls were amazingly pretty. I knew George's girl at once; she was at his side, his eyes shining as he towered over her.

We were there for half an hour, until the pinning and dressing were completed. The room a hothouse, everybody talked at once, and I could not understand a word, except when the black-eyed girl into whose charge I had been given by George interpreted for me. Finally there was a tremendous shouting up and down stairs and we all went out. A large truck with two benches inside was our transport to the hall.

We arrived in about ten minutes, in a hall festooned with flags and coloured paper decorations. At one end was a buffet, where one bought food and drink, at the other, on a dais, was a band. Its members were also in festive attire, red trousers with a white stripe, frogged hussar coats, hats with a peacock feather—the Cracovian costume. It was a string orchestra and played magnificently. There must have been two hundred people dancing on the floor. There was some jazz, but the folk dances predominated, with old-fashioned waltzes and polkas. The ensemble dances were great fun and a splendid sight. George and Gladys, my dark-eyed friend, would not let me stay out. Finally George, somewhere, procured what looked like a Paisley shawl, in which they draped me, completing the costume with a yellow curtain rope tied round my waist, and an American sailor's cap that had been dyed red. Thus attired I was pulled and bounced through Polish national dances, and sometimes, in the great swinging rondos, rode through the air. I confess I had never had such fun in my life. The dancing grew faster, the music louder. And then, like an old friend, I knew the music. We were dancing to one of Chopin's mazurkas!

We were not all Polish; there were some Russians, Lithuanians, Czechs and Germans. Here they were, all dancing joyously together. If they had been across the Atlantic they would all have been fighting each other. I noticed that in the dance hall nearly all spoke English. As soon as they were in groups they lapsed into their native tongues. * * *

At twelve o'clock the whole company stood still while the band played the Polish national anthem, and then "The Star-Spangled Banner." We all loitered, talking for a time. Then the truck took us back to the house. Upstairs in the parlour we gathered again, and the fat man, who owned the house and was apparently a capitalist, produced some bottles of champagne, made a passionate speech, which I was told was all about the mining town of Teschen, where he was born, which certainly the Czechs and the Austrians had never had any right to. He began to shout and perspire very much until the company started singing and drowned him. "What bad taste!" said Gladys. "He always makes it political."

At two o'clock we left the company, very much embraced, our hands very much shaken. I had learned Polish for "Thank you very much" and "I hope we shall meet again," which I repeated feelingly. What good, kind souls they were. In a few minutes we had changed. I had already shed my shawl and belt, and we were back in our travelling clothes. Half an hour later we were leaving Scranton asleep in the moonlight, heading for Bethlehem, on the edge of Pennsylvania, Newark in New Jersey, and New York. * * *

This was a world Hollywood seldom takes notice of and which only enters the novelist's survey in its most dramatic or violent aspects. It differed completely from the English scene. Racially I had been in "the melting pot" except, it seemed to me, that no real amalgam had followed the melting. The people were something new, and yet remained, even in the second and third generation, something old. They were American and Polish, American and German, American and Welsh, American and Irish. One would not doubt their Americanism, it was sturdy and demonstrative, but so also were their inherited racial traditions. I reflected that, in one sense, from Chicago to New York, I had made

Jonathan Raban
The Imaginary River 1981

HAD FIRST READ *HUCKLEBERRY FINN* when I was seven. The picture on its cover, crudely drawn and colored, supplied me with the raw material for an exquisite and recurrent daydream. It showed a boy alone, his face prematurely wizened with experience. (The artist hadn't risked his hand with the difficulties of bringing off a lifelike Nigger Jim.) The sheet of water on which he drifted was immense, an enameled pool of lapis lazuli. Smoke from a half-hidden steamboat hung over an island of Gothic conifers. Cut loose from the world, chewing on his corncob pipe, the boy was blissfully lost in this stillwater paradise.

For days I lay stretched out on the floor of my attic room, trying to bring the river to life from its code of print. It was tough going. Often I found Huck's American dialect as impenetrable as Latin, but even in the most difficult bits I was kept at it by the persistent wink and glimmer of the river. I was living inside the book. Because I was more timid and less sociable than Huck, his and my adventures on the Mississippi tended to diverge. He would sneak off in disguise to forage in a riverside town, or raid a wrecked steamboat; I would stay back on the raft. I laid trotlines for catfish. I floated alone on that unreal blue, watching for "towheads" and "sawyers" as the forest unrolled, a mile or more across the water.

I found the Mississippi in the family atlas. It was a great ink-stained Victorian book, almost as big as I was. "North Africa" and "Italy" had come loose from its binding, from my mother's attempts to keep up with my father's campaigns in the Eighth Army. North America, though, was virgin territory: no one in the family had ever thought the place worth a moment of their curiosity. I looked at the Mississippi, wriggling down the middle of the page, and liked the funny names of the places that it passed through. Just the sounds of Minneapolis . . . Dubuque . . . Hannibal . . . St. Louis . . . Cairo . . . Memphis . . . Natchez . . . Baton Rouge . . . struck a legendary and heroic note to my ear. Our part of England was culpably short of Roman generals, Indians and Egyptian ruins, and these splendid names added even more luster to the marvelous river in my head.

The only real river I knew was hardly more than a brook. It spilled through a tumbledown mill at the bottom of our road, opened into a little trouty pool, then ran on through water meadows over graveled shallows into Fakenham, where it slowed and deepened, gathering strength for the long drift across muddy flatlands to Norwich and the North Sea. All through my Huckleberry Finn summer, I came down to the mill to fish for roach and dace, and if I concentrated really hard, I could see the Mississippi there. First I had to think it twice as wide, then multiply by two, then two again . . . The rooftops of Fakenham went under. I sank roads, farms, church spires, the old German prisoner-of-war camp, Mr. Banham's flour mill. I flooded Norfolk, silvering the landscape like a mirror, leaving just an island here, a dead tree there, to break this lonely, enchanted monotony of water. It was a heady, intensely private vision. I hugged the idea of the huge river to myself. I exulted in the freedom and solitude of being afloat on it in my imagination.

Year by year I added new scraps of detail to the picture. I came across some photographs of the Mississippi in a dog-eared copy of the *National Geographic* in a doctor's waiting room. Like inefficient pornography, they were unsatisfying because they were too meanly explicit. "Towboat *Herman Briggs* at Greenville" and "Madrid Bend, Missouri" gave the river a set of measurements that I didn't at all care for. I didn't want to know that it was a mile and a quarter wide, or that its ruffled water wasn't blue at all but dirty tan. The lovely, immeasurable river in my head was traduced by these artless images, and when the doctor called me in to listen to the noises in my asthmatic chest I felt saved by the bell.

Then I saw a painting by George Caleb Bingham. It showed the Missouri, not the Mississippi, but I recognized it immediately as my river. Its water had a crystalline solidity and smoothness, as if it had been carved from rosy quartz. The river and the sky were one, with cliffs and forest hanging in suspension between them. In the foreground, a ruffianly trapper and his son drifted in a dugout canoe, their pet fox chained to its prow. The water captured their reflections as faithfully as a film. Alone, self-contained, they moved with the river, an integral part of the powerful current of things, *afloat* on it in exactly the way I had been daydreaming for myself. The French fur trader and his half-caste child joined Huck Finn—the three persons of the trinity which presided over my river.

Crouched under the willow below the mill, I lobbed my baited hook into the pool and watched the water spread. The Mississippi was my best invention; a dream that was always there, like a big friendly room with an open door into which I could wander at will. Once inside it, I was at home. I let the river grow around me until the world consisted of nothing except me and that great comforting gulf of water where catfish rootled and wild fruit hung from the trees on the tow-head islands. The river was completely still as the distant shore went inching by. I felt my skin burn in the sun. I smelled sawn timber and blackberries and persimmons. I didn't dare move a muscle for fear of waking from the dream. * * *

I hardly gave a thought to the mechanics of the voyage. It was, after all, a dream journey, and like a dream it was supposed to unfold spontaneously without effort on my part. Obviously I would need a craft of some kind, but I knew almost nothing at all about boats. A raft would turn the trip into a piece of quaint playacting; canoes capsized. I vaguely assumed that somewhere at the top end of the river

I'd come across a leaky tub with a pair of oars, and cast off in that.

To make the voyage come true, I began to talk about it. At a party in London I met a man who had seen the Mississippi at St. Louis and had gone on a half-day tourist cruise up the river.

"It was amazingly depressing," he said. "Totally featureless. An awful lot of mud. You couldn't see anything over the top of the banks except dead trees. The only bearable thing about the entire afternoon was the ship's bar. It was full of people getting dead drunk so that they didn't have to look at the sheer bloody boredom of the Mississippi."

"That was just around St. Louis, though."

"Oh, it's all like that, I gather. That's what it's famous for, being very long and very boring. The only reason people ever go on the Mississippi at all is because after you've spent a couple of hours looking at that horrendous bloody river, even a dump like St. Louis starts to look moderately interesting. I think God made the Mississippi as a sort of warning, to prove that things really can be worse than you think."

He had an air of mighty self-satisfaction, having delivered me at a stroke from the lunatic fantasy with which I'd been possessed. Actually, I'd been rather excited by his description of the river. It had given it something of the melodramatic awfulness of a landscape by John Martin, a touch of *Sadek in Search of the Waters of Oblivion* with its dwarfish hominid scrambling into a world of treeless crags and dead seas.

"I suppose you thought you were going to do it in a *rowing* boat," the man said, snuffling with amusement at the notion. I didn't like the way he had consigned my trip to the past subjunctive tense.

"No, no. I'll have a . . . an outboard motor." I had had one experience with an outboard motor. I had driven myself from one end of a small Scottish loch to the other, where it had coughed and died. It had taken me three hours to row back through a rainstorm.

"You'd get swamped. Or be run down by one of those tow-things. When we were in St. Louis, people were always getting drowned in the river. Went out fishing, never came back, bodies recovered weeks later, or never recovered at all. So bloody common that it hardly ever made the local news."

Some days afterward, I ran into the man again.

"You're not still thinking of going down that river, are you?"

"I've written off about getting a motor."

"It'd cost you a hell of a lot less if you just swallowed a packet of razor blades. According to the Euthanasia Society, putting a plastic bag over your head is pretty much the best way to go." He introduced me to the woman he was with. "He's going to go down the Mississippi in a *dinghy,*" he said.

"What a lovely thing to do," she said. "Just like Tom Sawyer—or was that Huckleberry Finn?"

The man smiled with exaggerated patience. It was the smile of a lonely realist stranded in the society of cloud-cuckoos.

☙*To get us started discovering what America is all about, British wit Oscar Wilde gives us some of his ironic impressions of America—its various beauties and lacks thereof.*

Oscar Wilde
Impressions of America 1882

I FEAR I CANNOT PICTURE AMERICA as altogether an Elysium—perhaps, from the ordinary standpoint I know but little about the country. I cannot give its latitude or longitude; I cannot compute the value of its dry goods, and I have no very close acquaintance with its politics. These are matters which may not interest you, and they certainly are not interesting to me.

The first thing that struck me on landing in America was that if the Americans are not the most well-dressed people in the world, they are the most comfortably dressed. Men are seen there with the dreadful chimney-pot hat, but there are very few hatless men; men wear the shocking swallow-tail coat, but few are to be seen with no coat at all. There is an air of comfort in the appearance of the people which is a marked contrast to that seen in this country, where, too often, people are seen in close contact with rags.

The next thing particularly noticeable is that everybody seems in a hurry to catch a train. This is a state of things which is not favourable to poetry or romance. Had Romeo or Juliet been in a constant state of anxiety about trains, or had their minds been agitated by the question of return-tickets, Shakespeare could not have given us those lovely balcony scenes which are so full of poetry and pathos.

America is the noisiest country that ever existed. One is waked up in the morning, not by the singing of the nightin-gale, but by the steam whistle. It is surprising that the sound practical sense of the Americans does not reduce this in-tolerable noise. All Art depends upon exquisite and delicate sensibility, and such continual turmoil must ultimately be destructive of the musical faculty.

There is not so much beauty to be found in American cities as in Oxford, Cambridge, Salisbury or Winchester, where are lovely relics of a beautiful age; but still there is a good deal of beauty to be seen in them now and then, but only where the American has not attempted to create it. Where the Americans have attempted to produce beauty they have signally failed. A remarkable characteristic of the Americans is the manner in which they have applied science to modern life.

This is apparent in the most cursory stroll through New York. In England an inventor is regarded almost as a crazy man, and in too many instances invention ends in disappointment and poverty. In America an inventor is honoured, help is forthcoming, and the exercise of ingenuity, the application of science to the work of man, is there the shortest road to wealth. There is no country in the world where machinery is so lovely as in America.

I have always wished to believe that the line of strength and the line of beauty are one. That wish was realized when I contemplated American machinery. It was not until I had seen the water-works at Chicago that I realized the wonders of machinery; the rise and fall of the steel rods, the symmetrical motion of the great wheels is the most beautifully rhythmic thing I have ever seen. One is impressed in America, but not favourably impressed, by the inordinate size of everything. The country seems to try to bully one into a belief in its power by its impressive bigness. * * *

It is in the colonies, and not in the mother country, that the old life of the country really exists. If one wants to realize what English Puritanism is—not at its worst (when it is very bad), but at its best, and then it is not very good—I do not think one can find much of it in England, but much can be found about Boston and Massachusetts. We have got rid of it. America still preserves it, to be, I hope, a short-lived curiosity.

San Francisco is a really beautiful city. China Town, peopled by Chinese labourers, is the most artistic town I have ever come across. The people—strange, melancholy Orientals, whom many people would call common, and they are certainly very poor—have determined that they will have nothing about them that is not beautiful. In the Chinese restaurant, where these navvies meet to have supper in the evening, I found them drinking tea out of china cups as delicate as the petals of a rose-leaf, whereas at the gaudy hotels I was supplied with a delf cup an inch and a half thick. When the Chinese bill was presented it was made out on rice paper, the account being done in Indian ink as fantastically as if an artist had been etching little birds on a fan. * * *

From Salt Lake City one travels over great plains of Colorado and up the Rocky Mountains, on the top of which is Leadville, the richest city in the world. It has also got the reputation of being the roughest, and every man carries a revolver. I was told that if I went there they would be sure to shoot me or my travelling manager. I wrote and told them that nothing that they could do to my travelling manager would intimidate me. They are miners—men working in metals, so I lectured them on the Ethics of Art. I read them passages from the autobiography of Benvenuto Cellini and they seemed much delighted. I was reproved by my hearers for not having brought him with me. I explained that he had been dead for some little time which elicited the enquiry 'Who shot him?' They afterwards took me to a dancing saloon where I saw the only rational method of art criticism I have ever come across. Over the piano was printed a notice:

Please do not shoot the pianist.
He is doing his best.

The mortality among pianists in that place is marvellous. Then they asked me to supper, and having accepted, I had to descend a mine in a rickety bucket in which it was impossible to be graceful. Having got into the heart of the mountain I had supper, the first course being whisky, the second whisky and the third whisky. * * *

Among the more elderly inhabitants of the South I found a melancholy tendency to date every event of importance by the late war. 'How beautiful the moon is tonight,' I once remarked to a gentleman who was standing next to me. 'Yes,' was his reply, 'but you should have seen it before the war.'

So infinitesimal did I find the knowledge of Art, west of the Rocky Mountains, that an art patron—one who in his day had been a miner—actually sued the railroad company for damages because the plaster cast of Venus of Milo, which he had imported from Paris, had been delivered minus the arms. And, what is more surprising still, he gained his case and the damages.

Pennsylvania, with its rocky gorges and woodland scenery, reminded me of Switzerland. The prairie reminded me of a piece of blotting-paper.

The Spanish and French have left behind them memorials in the beauty of their names. All the cities that have beautiful names derive them from the Spanish or the French. The English people give intensely ugly names to places. One place had such an ugly name that I refused to lecture there. It was called Grigsville. Supposing I had founded a school of Art there—fancy 'Early Grigsville'. Imagine a School of Art teaching 'Grigsville Renaissance'.

As for slang I did not hear much of it, though a young lady who had changed her clothes after an afternoon dance did say that 'after the heel kick she had shifted her day goods'.

American youths are pale and precocious, or sallow and supercilious, but American girls are pretty and charming—little oases of pretty unreasonableness in a vast desert of practical common-sense.

Every American girl is entitled to have twelve young men devoted to her. They remain her slaves and she rules them with charming nonchalance. * * *

In going to America one learns that poverty is not a necessary accompaniment to civilization. There at any rate is a country that has no trappings, no pageants and no gorgeous ceremonies. I saw only two processions—one was the Fire Brigade preceded by the Police, the other was the Police preceded by the Fire Brigade.

Voluntary immigrants since the days of Columbus have seen America as a fantasyland of gold and, if not ambrosia, hamburgers at least. And once they establish themselves here, the fantasies turn into that ravenous creature of fiction and drama, the American Dream.

Nothing is more American than the American Dream. But it is not something that simply walks up and shakes an American's hand; Americans have to go out and seek it. Which means they've got to travel. In the following parody of American literature, Ian Frazier, one of America's best young humorists, drives off in a parodic journey into the American Dream.

Ian Frazier
Into the American Maw   1986

I WAS DRIVING BACK TO NEW YORK from Boston last Sunday and I stopped in a restaurant to get something to eat, and as I sat there waiting for my order to come, looking at my ice water and my silverware and the paper placemat, suddenly something struck me: I just might be on a savage nightmare journey to the heart of the American dream! I wasn't sure exactly what savage nightmare journeys to the heart of the American dream required, but I knew that since America has a love affair with the automobile, it was probably difficult to pursue a nightmare journey on public transportation. Fortunately, I had my own car, a 1970 Maverick. Beyond that, I couldn't think of any hard-and-fast requirements, so I decided that I *was* on a savage journey to the heart of the American dream, and I was glad that it was a Sunday. That made it more convenient for me. Once I had accepted this possibility, it was amazing how I saw all of America in a new light. Insights started coming to me one after the other, and I decided to reveal them in a voice as flat and affectless as the landscape that surrounded me (I was in a relatively flat part of Connecticut at the time).

First, I realized that discount stores—you know, the discount stores you see all over the place in America—well, I realized that discount stores equal emptiness. Beyond that, I realized that different discount stores represent different shades of emptiness—Caldor's equals an emptiness tinged with a sad, ineffable sense of mourning for a lost American innocence, while Brands Mart equals an emptiness much closer to what European philosophers call "anomie," and Zayre's equals an emptiness along the lines of Sartre's "nausea." Next, I realized that the interstate highway system equals nihilism. Have you ever been on Interstate 75 north of Berea, Kentucky? If you have, you know the stretch I'm thinking of—it's one of the most nihilistic stretches of four-lane possibly in the whole world. Although there certainly are lots of nihilistic interstate highways in every state in this country. In California, every stretch of road—I don't care whether it's interstate or a state highway or a county road or gravel or asphalt or oil—all of it is nihilistic.

Thinking about California led me to dizzying thoughts about L.A.—L.A., where sometimes on the signs advertising used-car lots they actually spell "car" with a "k." . . . L.A., a place that is so different from the East Coast. New York City, of course, is a woman. In fact, the entire tristate area, including New York, Connecticut, and New Jersey, is a woman. But L.A.—L.A. is the City of the One-Night Stands. Or at least that's what I had heard. Just to be sure, I decided to call L.A. long-distance, my voice crying through wires across the vast, buffalo-scarred dreamscape of a haunted republic. I told L.A. that I was coming out for four days, and could I possibly get a three-night stand. They said no, sir. They said I had to get three one-night stands. Q.E.D.

I paid my check and left the restaurant and got in my car. Luckily, it started. I began to drive—to drive to nowhere on a vast blank ribbon, to drive without direction or purpose (beyond getting home sometime that evening), surrounded by other Americans, my partners in the dream, all of them sealed off from me and each other by metal and glass. It got dark and began to rain, and still I was driving. I turned on the windshield wipers, and it wasn't long before I saw in the windshield the images of all my fathers before me. I saw my great-great-grandfathers' faces—not all eight of my great-great-grandfathers' faces but, say, maybe five of them—and then I saw my great-grandfathers and my grandfathers and my father, and all the faces merged into my face, reflected in the blue light from the dashboard as the wipers swished back and forth. And then my face changed into the faces of people who I guess were supposed to be my descendants. And still I was driving, stopping only occasionally to pay either thirty cents or twenty-five cents for tolls. I was on that stretch of 95 where you have to pay tolls every ten miles or so.

I stopped at a gas station to buy cigarettes. I put eighty cents in change into the machine, and pulled the knob for my brand—Camel Lights. Nothing came out. Then I pulled the knob for Vantage. Nothing came out. Then I pushed the coin return, and nothing came out. Then I pulled all of the other knobs, and nothing came out—a metaphor.

One of the strangest things about America is the fact that while everyone the world over seems to be resenting the Americanization of their culture, it takes a great effort to try to find something American in America to take foreign visitors to see or do. After all, we are a melting pot, and melting pots don't have a lot of character. Imagine a fondue of camembert, cheddar, feta, and gorgonzola with a few shakes each of cumin, coriander, ginger, and paprika tossed on. It doesn't quite make your mouth water. In the following selection, American writer Mary McCarthy tries to come up with an American place to take a French visitor.

Mary McCarthy
A Really American Place 1947

A VISITING EXISTENTIALIST wanted recently to be taken to dinner at a really American place. This proposal, natural enough in a tourist, disclosed a situation thoroughly unnatural. Unless the visiting lady's object was suffering, there was no way of satisfying her demand. Sukiyaki joints, chop suey joints, Italian table d'hote places, French provincial restaurants with the menu written on a slate, Irish chophouses, and Jewish delicatessens came abundantly to mind, but these were not what the lady wanted. Schrafft's or the Automat would have answered, yet to take her there would have been to turn oneself into a tourist and to present America as a spectacle—a *New Yorker* cartoon or a savage drawing in the *New Masses*. It was the beginning of an evening of humiliations. The visitor was lively and eager; her mind lay open and orderly, like a notebook ready for impressions. It was not long, however, before she shut it up with a snap. We had no recommendations to make to her. With movies, plays, current books, it was the same story as with the restaurants. *Open City, Les Enfants du Paradis,* Oscar Wilde, a reprint of Henry James were *paté de maison* to this lady who wanted the definitive flapjack. She did not believe us when we said that there were no good Hollywood movies, no good Broadway plays—only curios; she was merely confirmed in her impression that American intellectuals were "negative."

Yet the irritating thing was that we did not feel negative. We admired and liked our country; we preferred it to that imaginary America, land of the *peaux rouges* of Caldwell and Steinbeck, dumb paradise of violence and the detective story, which had excited the sensibilities of our visitor and of the up-to-date French literary world. But to found our preference, to locate it materially in some admirable object or institution, such as Chartres, say, or French cafe life, was for us, that night at any rate, an impossible undertaking. We heard ourselves saying that the real America was elsewhere, in the white frame houses and church spires of New England; yet we knew that we talked foolishly—we were not Granville Hicks and we looked ludicrous in his opinions. The Elevated, half a block away, interrupting us every time a train passed, gave us the lie on schedule, every eight minutes. But if the elm-shaded village green was a false or at least an insufficient address for the *genius loci* we honored, where then was it to be found? Surveyed from the vantage point of Europe, this large continent seemed suddenly deficient in objects of virtue. The Grand Canyon, Yellowstone Park, Jim Hill's mansion in St. Paul, Jefferson's Monticello, the blast furnaces of Pittsburgh, Mount Rainier, the yellow observatory at Amherst, the little-theatre movement in Cleveland, Ohio, a Greek revival house glimpsed from a car window in a lost river-town in New Jersey—these things were too small for the size of the country. Each of them, when pointed to, diminished in interest with the lady's perspective of distance. There was no sight that in itself seemed to justify her crossing of the Atlantic.

If she was interested in "conditions," that was a different matter. There are conditions everywhere; it takes no special genius to produce them. Yet would it be an act of hospitality to invite a visitor to a lynching? Unfortunately, nearly all the "sights" in America fall under the head of conditions. Hollywood, Reno, the sharecroppers' homes in the South, the mining towns of Pennsylvania, Coney Island, the Chicago stockyards, Macy's, the Dodgers, Harlem, even Congress, the forum of our liberties, are spectacles rather than sights, to use the term in the colloquial sense of "Didn't he make a holy spectacle of himself?" An Englishman of almost any political opinion can show a visitor through the Houses of Parliament with a sense of pride or at least of indulgence toward his national foibles and traditions. The American, if he has a spark of national feeling, will be humiliated by the difficulties, for nearly everything that is beautiful and has not been produced by nature belongs to the eighteenth century, to a past with which he has very little connection, and which his ancestors, in many or most cases, had no part in. Beacon Street and the Boston Common are very charming in the eighteenth-century manner, so are the sea captains' houses in the old Massachusetts ports, and the ruined plantations of Louisiana, but an American from Brooklyn or the Middle West or the Pacific Coast finds the style of life embodied in them as foreign as Europe; indeed, the first sensation of a Westerner, coming upon Beacon Hill and the gold dome of the State House, is to feel that at last he has traveled "abroad." The American, if he is to speak the highest truth about his country, must refrain from pointing at all. The virtue of American civilization is that it is unmaterialistic.

Mircea Vasiliu. By permission of the artist.

❧Accommodations

❧*Although they're only places to hang our hats (and put up our worn-out feet), hotels are some of the most memorable parts of any journey and certainly one of the things we like to complain about the most. And even with the internationalization of the hotel chain, the hotel is often the place where we see foreign (or local) practices up closest.*

Classic American humorist Robert Benchley takes a topsy-turvy look at the American hotel, and American essayist Noel Perrin's looks smilingly at the meaning of the revered American country inn.

Robert Benchley
The Homelike Hotel   1930

ONE OF THE CHIEF FACTORS in the impending crash of the American Home as an institution is the present craze for making so many other places "homelike." We have homelike hotels, homelike barber shops, homelike auditoriums, and, so they tell me, homelike jails. A man can't go into a shop to get his skates sharpened without being made to feel that, if he has any appreciation for atmosphere at all, he ought really to send for his trunks and settle down and live right there in the skate-sharpening place. It is getting so that a home-loving man doesn't know which way to turn.

The hotels were the leaders in this campaign to make the home seem unhomelike by comparison. There was a time when a hotel was simply a place in which you slept; that is, if you were a good sleeper. You went in and registered and the man who pushed the book out at you turned his collar around and became the boy who took your bag up (possibly in one of those new-fangled lifts which you were sure would never replace the horse—at least, not in your affections).

The room, as you entered it, seemed to be a species of closet, smelling strongly of straw matting and rug threads, and, after a good look at the cherry bureau and its duplicating mirror and a tug at the rope which was coiled by the window in case you wanted to lasso any one, you turned out the hanging bulb over the bed (making a barely perceptible difference in the lighting of the room), and went out into the street to find a place to sit until bedtime. You would no more have thought of sitting in your room than you would have thought of getting into one of the bureau drawers and lolling around with a good book.

The first sign that the hotels were going in for the homey stuff in a big way was when they began hanging pictures on the walls. Either they didn't get the right pictures or they weren't hung properly. At any rate, the first hotel wall pictures were not successful in giving a homelike atmosphere. There were usually pastels showing two ladies with a fan, or two fans and one lady, with a man in knee breeches hovering about in the background. The girl with the broken jug was also a great favorite in the early days of hotel decoration. She still is doing very well, as a matter of fact, and you will find her in even the most up-to-date hostelries, giving what is hoped will be a final touch of bonhomie to the room. Well, she doesn't, and the sooner hotel managements are brought to realize it, the better it will be for them.

In fact, the whole problem of what pictures to hang on the walls of a hotel room is still in a state of flux. Until they get away from those little French garden scenes, with fans and sun dials as the chief props, they are never going to make me feel at home. And they do not help matters any by introducing etchings showing three boats lying alongside a dock or 17 geese flying South. It seems to me that the picture-hangers in hotels are striving too hard for good taste. What we want is not good taste in our hotel pictures, but something to look at. If you are going to live in the room with a picture all the rest of your life, good taste is all right. But for overnight give me something a little daring, with a lot of red in it.

There is another development in the equipment of hotel rooms which, while it does not exactly make the quarters attractive, keeps the guest interested while he is in the room. I refer to the quantity of reading matter which is placed at his disposal. This does not mean the little magazines that some hotels place by the bedside, in the hope that you will sit up so late reading that you will have to send down for a glass of milk and some crackers at midnight. I don't think people read those as much as they are supposed to. I don't think they even look at the pictures as much as they are supposed to.

But there is a trait which is almost universal among hotel guests and which is being catered to more and more by the managements. It is the tendency, amounting almost to a fascination, to read every word of every sign which is displayed around the room. You know very well that the chances are that not one sign out of ten will have any bearing on you or your life in that room. And yet, almost as soon as the bellboy has left, you amble around the room, reading little notices which have been slipped under the glass bureau top, tacked to the door, or tucked in the mirror. Not only do you read them once, but you usually go over them a second time, hoping that maybe there is something of interest which eluded you in the first reading.

I had occasion last week to share a hotel room with a man who was at Atlantic City with me on business. We were shown up by the boy, who went through all the regulation manoeuvres of opening the window (which has to be shut immediately after he has gone), putting the bags on the stool (from which they have to be removed for unpacking), pushing open the door to the bathroom to show you where it is and to prevent your going into the next room by mistake, and making such financial adjustments as may be necessary. This completed, I reminded George that we were already late for our first appointment, and started for the door to go downstairs.

George, however, was busy at something over by the bureau. "Just a minute," he said, in a preoccupied tone. He was bending over the glass top as if he had found a deposit of something that might possibly turn out to be gold.

Impatiently I went over to grab him by the arm and pull him along. I saw he was reading a little notice, printed in red, which had been tucked under the glass. Determined to see what this fascinating message was that had riveted George to the spot, I read:

The use of alcohol lamps, sterno lamps, and all other flame-producing appliances, as well as electric devices, is positively forbidden.

"That makes it rather tough for you, doesn't it," I said, "with all your flame-producing appliances? Shall we go to another hotel?"

George said nothing, but went to get his hat. I sauntered over to the door to wait for him, but my eye was caught by a neatly-printed sign which, although I knew that it would contain nothing which could possibly affect me personally, I was utterly unable to keep from reading:

In accepting garments for valet service it is thoroughly understood that they do not contain money, jewelry, or any other articles of value, and, consequently ——

"Come on, come on!" said George. "We're late now!"

"Just a minute!" It was I this time who had the preoccupied air. It was I whose eyes were glued to the tiny card and who could not leave until I had finished its stirring message——

—consequently the hotel's management or any of its staff will not be held responsible for the return of anything but the garments originally delivered.

"O.K.!" I announced briskly. "Come on!"

But George had found another sign on the wall by the door. This time we both read it together in silence.

Do not turn thumb latch when leaving room. Door is self-locking. Use thumb latch only when in room.

"What thumb latch is that?" George said, looking over the assortment of latches and catches on the door.

"This is it here," I said, equally engrossed.

"Don't turn it!" cried George, in terror. "It says not to turn it."

"Who's turning it?" I snapped back. "I was just seeing how it worked. Who would want to turn it, anyway?"

"You can't tell," replied George. "Somebody might have this room who had a terrible hunch for turning thumb latches. A hotel has to deal with a lot of strange eggs."

"What would happen if you did turn it?" I asked.

George shuddered. "It might transform the whole hotel into a pumpkin under our very feet," he said, in a low voice.

"Don't be so jumpy," I said, impatiently. "That sort of thing belongs to the Middle Ages—and, besides, it used to happen only at the stroke of midnight."

"What time is it now?" asked George. He was in a cold sweat.

"A quarter to five," I said, looking at my watch. "There's not much sense in going to that four-o'clock date now."

George agreed, so we took off our hats and spent the rest of the afternoon roaming about the room, reading signs to our hearts' content. We were rewarded by several even duller notices than the ones we had already studied and by a good 15 minutes over the 21 provisions of Act 146 of the state Legislature making it compulsory for the management of all inns, hotels, and boarding houses to maintain a safe in the office for the reception of valuables belonging to the guests.

"That's an old one," said George. "I've read that before."

"It's good, though," I said. "It always makes great reading. After all, old notices are best."

So we had dinner sent up to the room in order to com-

We spent the rest of the afternoon reading signs to our hearts' content

Gluyas Williams. By permission of Joyce W. Williams.

plete our reading of the hotel laundry list (George flying into a rage at the charge of 75 cents for "dressing sacques") and, by bedtime, had cleaned up the entire supply of printed matter and were well into the Atlantic City telephone book.

If the hotels want to go still further in their campaigns to make their rooms interesting for their guests, I would suggest the introduction of a sort of treasure hunt for each room. On each door could be tacked a little legend saying something like: "I can be found by going (1) to the top of the possession of an old English queen (2) under an article, beginning with 'W,' highly prized by astronomers (3) between two Indian wigwam attachments (4) underneath an American revolutionary firearm."

The guest could then spend his evenings trying to figure out these hiding places and perhaps emerge richer by a cigarette lighter or one of those face cloths done up in tissue paper envelopes which the hotels are so crazy to have you take away. It wouldn't be so much the value of the prize as the fun of finding it, and it would serve the purpose which seems to be the aim of all modern hostelries—namely: to keep the guests out of the open air and to prevent them from going home.

Noel Perrin
A Sign of Friendship 1978

THERE IS A HIGHWAY SIGN I sometimes pass in Connecticut which asserts that there are eight friendly inns on a body of water called Lake Waramaug and urges me to stay at one of them. In mere reality it would be difficult to ask that sign how friendliness can be offered as a commodity, like clean towels or room service. For the dweller in fantasy it's a snap. The last time by I had a chat with it which went something like this:

ME: Hello, you friendly sign.

SIGN: *(friendlily)* Hello-alo. That's a nice car you're driving, Mister. I like you. Why don't you take your next left and come on to Lake Waramaug?

ME: Maybe I will. Are all eight of the inns really friendly?

SIGN: Are they? Why, Mister, you don't know what friendship means till you've stayed at Lake Waramaug.

ME: *(suddenly, at 39, struck by doubts)* By gosh, you're right. I don't know. What does friendship mean?

SIGN: At our inns, it means that everybody from the bellhop to the manager is sincerely glad to see you, that we have a relaxed, friendly atmosphere—

ME: Hold it. You can't define a word in terms of itself.

SIGN: Oops. I mean a relaxed, *casual* atmosphere where everything's very informal, where the bartender smiles as he mixes you a martini, where, well, where everybody from the bellhop to the manager is sincerely glad to see you.

ME: That's great! I love big welcomes. We'll all be real friends, right?

SIGN: *(after a second's hesitation)* Sure. Every guest is a friend.

ME: Sign, this is the best news I've had in a long time. It just happens that I'm dead tired, dead broke, and very hungry. A clean bed and a good dinner are just what I need. Which of my new friends shall I stay with?

SIGN: *(icy cold)* Listen, buddy, if you're looking for charity, why don't you try the Traveler's Aid?

ME: When I've got sincere friends all around Lake Waramaug? Why should I?

SIGN: OK, I walked into that one. So they're not your real friends.

ME: But they're still sincerely glad to see me?

SIGN: Well, yes, sure. What I meant was that provided you can pay your bill, everybody from the bellhop to the manager feels sincerely glad to see you, whether they personally like you or not; and any employee that can't feel that way gets fired. Fair enough?

70

ME: You mean you have to be a hypocrite to work at Lake Waramaug?

SIGN: Look, I'm just a sign, and I'm ten miles back on the road as it is. Why don't you go talk to the man that wrote me?

✒*There's really not too much to be said for American cuisine. Yes, we've certainly got a lot of great ethnic restaurants, more than anywhere else. But what we really have to show for ourselves is the fast-food restaurant, the diner, and the plague of the traveler, the tourist spot. British travel writer Margaret Powell takes a glance at the Olde English variety of the tourist spot, and then John Steinbeck finds the essence of New England in a roadside diner. To finish this section off, nineteenth-century American humorist Bill Nye tells us how American waiters got their name.*

Margaret Powell
An Olde Pub 1973

BACK IN OUR HOTEL we decided to have a drink in what the management termed 'The Old English Pub, a charming replica of an old country pub'. The waiters were attired in a sort of loose white blouse, red waistcoat and breeches, and tight white leggings to the knees. What particular period of British history this gear was meant to represent was a mystery to me. Was it ever a period of British history? Perhaps the old coaching inns. Maybe the barmen were redolent of 'ye olde worlde', but not much else was. The seats were upholstered in some kind of plastic material, and, to add to the incongruity, a television set was over the bar and a long row of people sitting on stools were gazing at it without saying a word. Where was the atmosphere of an old English pub! In retrospect it was just like any American bar apart from the different decor. It's people that make a pub—those who own it, those who serve and their customers.

I just couldn't imagine an American barman waiting on the customers with the same kind of service that one gets in a real old English pub—not that there are so many of them left now. Where was the conversation? The 'Good evening! Lovely weather for the time of the year.' Here the barman came to our table, stood there without saying a word, took our order, brought it to us and walked off. He would be about as much at home in a country pub as I would be in an igloo.

John Steinbeck
Break Fast, Not Silence 1962

SOON DISCOVERED that if a wayfaring stranger wishes to eavesdrop on a local population the places for him to slip in and hold his peace are bars and churches. But some New England towns don't have bars, and church is only on Sunday. A good alternative is the roadside restaurant where men gather for breakfast before going to work or going hunting. To find these places inhabited, one must get up very early. And there is a drawback even to this. Early-rising men not only do not talk much to strangers, they barely talk to one another. Breakfast conversation is limited to a series of laconic grunts. The natural New England taciturnity reaches its glorious perfection at breakfast.

I fed Charley, gave him a limited promenade, and hit the road. An icy mist covered the hills and froze on my windshield. I am not normally a breakfast eater, but here I had to be or I wouldn't see anybody unless I stopped for gas. At the first lighted roadside restaurant I pulled in and took my seat at a counter. The customers were folded over their coffee cups like ferns. A normal conversation is as follows:

WAITRESS: "Same?"

CUSTOMER: "Yep."

WAITRESS: "Cold enough for you?"

CUSTOMER: "Yep."

(Ten minutes.)

WAITRESS: "Refill?"

CUSTOMER: "Yep."

This is a really talkative customer. Some reduce it to "Burp" and others do not answer at all. An early morning waitress in New England leads a lonely life, but I soon learned that if I tried to inject life and gaiety into her job with a blithe remark she dropped her eyes and answered "Yep" or "Umph." Still, I did feel that there was some kind of communication, but I can't say what it was.

Bill Nye
That's Why They Call
'Em '*Wait*ers' 1886

FROM THE TARDY AND POLISHED LOITERER of the effete East, to the off-hand and social equal of the budding West, all waiters are deserving of philosophical scrutiny. I was thrown in contact with a waiter in New York last summer, whose manners were far more polished than my own. Every time I saw him standing there with his immediate pantaloons and swallow-tail coat, and the far-away, chastened look of one who had been unfortunate, but not crushed, I felt that I was unworthy to be waited upon by such a blue-blooded thoroughbred, and I often wished that we had more such men in Congress. And when he would take my order and go away with it, and after the meridian of my life had softened into the mellow glory of the sere and yellow leaf, when he came back, still looking quite young, and never having forgotten me, recognizing me readily after the long, dull, desolate years, I was glad, and I felt that he deserved something more than mere empty thanks and I said to him: "Ah, sir, you still remember me after years of privation and suffering. When every one else in New York has forgotten me, with the exception of the confidence man, you came to me with the glad light of recognition in your clear eye. Would you be offended if I gave you this trifling testimonial of my regard?" at the same time giving him my note at thirty days.

I wanted him to have something by which to always remember me, and I guess he has.

"America is too democratic a country to have good service."

C.V.R. Thompson

❧Transportation

❧*Transportation may not be the essence of travel, but you can't very well travel without it. Or at least not very far. Especially in the U. S. of A.*

The U.S. has a lot of miles to cover, but mileage is not really an accurate measure of travel distances. When you say that a drive from New York to Los Angeles is 3,000 miles, you've said very little. When you say it takes 54 hours at the official speed limit (or at the usual speed with stops for meals), you've said more. But when you say that your children can sing almost 7,500 verses of "Ninety-nine Bottles of Beer on the Wall" on one cross-country drive, you can get a clear idea of how incredibly monotonous the trip can be and decide that a plane ticket might be cheaper than the shrink you'll need when you get home.

As big as the U.S. is, the transportation of choice is still the automobile. Perhaps it's just that leaving the driving to others means missing all the fun: the fights over directions, the breakdowns, and the lost sleep. Whatever the advantages of driving—freedom, getting off the beaten track, not having strangers fall asleep on your shoulder—they seem to outweigh the disadvantages.

To shed some light on driving through America, we have American novelist John Steinbeck on roadmaps, Minnesotan expert Howard Mohr on asking directions, British-American humorist Bill Bryson on driving with children, and Israel's leading humorist Ephraim Kishon on the country gas station that is far more than just a place to fill your tank.

John Steinbeck
Like Starting a Novel 1962

FOR WEEKS I HAD STUDIED MAPS, large-scale and small, but maps are not reality at all—they can be tyrants. I know people who are so immersed in road maps that they never see the countryside they pass through, and others who, having traced a route, are held to it as though held by flanged wheels to rails. I pulled Rocinante into a small picnic area maintained by the state of Connecticut and got out my book of maps. And suddenly the United States became huge beyond belief and impossible ever to cross. I wondered how in hell I'd got myself mixed up in a project that couldn't be carried out. It was like starting to write a novel. When I face the desolate impossibility of writing five hundred pages a sick sense of failure falls on me and I know I can never do it. This happens every time. Then gradually I write one page and then another. One day's work is all I can permit myself to contemplate and I eliminate the possibility of ever finishing. So it was now, as I looked at the bright-colored projection of monster America.

Howard Mohr
Asking Directions in Minnesota 1987

IF YOU NEED DIRECTIONS on a motoring tour through rural Minnesota, simply stop the car when you see a Minnesotan and speak through your rolled-down driver's window. If the directions get involved—which is very likely—you can get out and stretch your legs. Nearly 50 percent of Minnesota conversations are conducted through the side window of a car or pickup or while leaning on the fender or hood, 30 percent are conducted over a little lunch at the kitchen table, 15 percent in a rowboat, and the remaining 5 percent take place in movie theaters during the movie. According to a recent study.

Words and Phrases

✓ I think I took a wrong turn.
✓ Howda ya git ta?
✓ Run that by me again, would you?

Dialogue Practice

DRIVER: "Say, howda ya git ta the Anderson farm? I think we took a wrong turn."

MINNESOTAN: "I figured something was up—this is your fourth time by and the sightseeing ain't the greatest here, unless you count my brother-in-law, but he don't get out much. Which way'd you come in?"

D: "From the north, I think. We went by this house with old tires in the front yard and the windows boarded up. It looked like it'd been struck by a high wind."

M: "It was, in '79. Some people said it was a tornado. That's where I live. I been meanin' to fix it up. So it wasn't north—you came in from the south."

D: "Does it matter?"

M: "Not to me it don't. But if you want to get where you're going, it does. Did you see the elevator?"

[Note: This is the grain elevator, which is several stories taller than everything else in small towns except maybe the water tower. It's where corn, soybeans, oats, and wheat are elevated and stored until they are shipped out in boxcars or trucks, and it's where all directions start. —H.M.]

M: "Okay, so, you go past the elevator then, on the blacktop. There is a gravel road there, but don't take it, take the blacktop until it comes to a tee where the welding shop used to be. It's just a field now. I think it's got corn in it this year. Ya go left there. You could go right there, but it'd be longer. A lot of people go that way, but I wouldn't. Ya go left then for, oh, say, I don't know, half a mile, three-quarters, maybe. It's just before the road dips where the sewage lagoon flooded last fall. You can't miss it. You take a left and go past the Pepper place—nobody lives there now. Past the big grove of dead elms. The next place is the Anderson farm, that's Orv Anderson. He married the oldest Peterson girl. That's Peter Peterson. Not Jack Peterson. He never had any kids, Jack didn't. The place after that is Arnie Anderson's. Orv and Arnie are brothers. Sven was their father. But if you're looking for the Olaf Andersons, then that's another matter. Remember the elevator? Well, take that gravel road south around Dead Gopher Lake. You can't miss it."

D: "Run that by me again, would you?"

Bill Bryson
Pleese! 1989

IN THE MORNING I rejoined Highway 127 south. This was marked on my map as a scenic route and for once this proved to be so. It really was attractive countryside, better than anything I knew Illinois possessed, with rolling hills of wine-bottle green, prosperous-looking farms and deep woods of oak and beech. Surprisingly, considering I was heading south, the foliage here was more autumnal than elsewhere—the hillsides were a mixture of mustard, dull orange and pale green, quite fetching—and the clear, sunny air had an agreeable crispness to it. I could live here, in these hills, I thought.

It took me a while to figure out what was missing. It was billboards. When I was small, billboards thirty feet wide and fifteen feet high stood in fields along every roadside. In places like Iowa and Kansas they were about the only stimulation you got. In the 1960s Lady Bird Johnson, in one of those misguided campaigns in which presidents' wives are always engaging themselves, had most of the roadside billboards removed as part of a highway beautification program. In the middle of the Rocky Mountains this was doubtless a good thing, but out here in the lonesome heartland billboards were practically a public service. Seeing one standing a mile off you would become interested to see what it said, and would watch with mild absorption as it advanced towards you and passed. As roadside excitements went, it was about on a par with the little windmills in Pella, but it was better than nothing.

The superior billboards would have a three-dimensional element to them—the head of a cow jutting out if it was for a dairy, or a cutout of a bowling ball scattering pins if it was for a bowling alley. Sometimes the billboard would be for some coming attraction. There might be a figure of a ghost and words, VISIT SPOOK CAVERNS! OKLAHOMA'S GREAT FAMILY ATTRACTION! JUST 69 MILES! A couple of miles later there would be another sign saying, PLENTY OF FREE PARKING AT SPOOK CAVERNS. JUST 67 MILES! And so it would go with sign after sign promising the most thrilling and instructive afternoon any family could ever hope to have, at least in Oklahoma. These promises would be supported by illustrations showing eerily lit underground chambers, the size of cathedrals, in which the stalactites and stalagmites had magically fused into the shapes of witches' houses, bubbling caldrons, flying bats and Casper the Friendly Ghost. It all looked extremely promising. So we children in the back would begin suggesting that we stop and have a look, taking it in turns to say, in a sincere and moving way, "Oh, *please,* Dad, oh, pleeeeease."

Over the next sixty miles my father's position on the matter would proceed through a series of well-worn phrases, beginning with a flat refusal on the grounds that it was bound to be expensive and anyway our behavior since breakfast had been so disgraceful that it didn't warrant any special treats, to studiously ignoring our pleas (this phase would last for up to eleven minutes), to asking my mother privately in a low voice what she thought about the idea and receiving an equivocal answer, to ignoring us again in the evident hope that we would forget about it and stop nagging (one minute, twelve seconds), to saying that we *might* go if we started to behave and kept on behaving more or less forever, to saying that we definitely would *not* go because, just look at us, we were already squabbling again and we hadn't even gotten there, finally announcing—sometimes in an exasperated bellow, sometimes in a deathbed whisper—that all right we would go. You could always tell when Dad was on the brink of acceptance because his neck would turn red. It was always the same. He always said yes in the end. I never understood why he didn't just accede to our demands at the outset and save himself thirty minutes of anguish. Then he would always quickly add, "But we're only going for half an hour—and you're not going to buy anything. Is that clear?" This seemed to restore to him a sense that he was in charge of things.

By the last two or three miles, the signs for Spook Caverns would be every couple of hundred yards, bringing us to a fever pitch of excitement. Finally there would be a billboard the size of a battleship with a huge arrow telling us to turn right here and drive eighteen miles. "Eighteen miles!" Dad would cry shrilly, his forehead veins stirring to life in preparation for the inevitable discovery that after eighteen miles of bouncing down a dirt road with knee-deep ruts there would be no sign of Spook Caverns, that indeed after nineteen miles the road would end in a desolate junction without any clue of which way to turn, and that Dad would turn the wrong way. When eventually found, Spook Caverns would prove to be rather less than advertised—in fact, would give every appearance of being in the last stages of solvency. The caverns, damp and ill lit and smelling like a long-dead horse, would be about the size of a garage and the stalactites and stalagmites wouldn't look the least bit like witches' houses and Casper the Ghost. They would look like—well, like stalactites and stalagmites. It would all be a huge letdown. The only possible way of assuaging our disappointment, we would discover, would be if Dad bought us each a rubber Bowie knife and bag of toy dinosaurs in the adjoining gift shop. My sister and I would drop to the ground and emit mournful noises to remind him what a fearful thing unassuaged grief can be in a child.

So, as the sun sank over the brown flatness of Oklahoma and Dad, hours behind schedule, embarked on the difficult business of not being able to find a room for the night (ably assisted by my mother, who would misread the maps and mistakenly identify almost every passing building as a possible motel), we children would pass the time in back by having noisy and vicious knife fights, breaking off at intervals to weep, report wounds and complain of hunger, boredom and the need for toilet facilities. It was a kind of living hell. And now there appeared to be almost no billboards along the highways. What a sad loss.

Ephraim Kishon
The All-Purpose Gas Station   1965

'WANT SOME ANTS?' The question was quite logical, but it aroused a certain amount of panic in us. Our approach to the race of industrious ants is definitely positive, being, as they are, most trade union conscious insects, and we leave them strictly alone as long as they don't bore into our kitchen through the walls. But did we want ants in a gas station sixty-four miles north of New York on the state highway? God knows. We therefore replied to the gasoline dispenser, who filled up the tank of our car:

'I beg your pardon?'

'I got a few more boxes left,' the attendant explained and wiped the windshield of our car in a show of goodwill. 'It's the fashion now. Fascinating ant farm. Fun for the whole family. The kids love to look through the glass at the ants building roads, bridges, subways. The whole thing works out at only $2.50. At the grocery you'd pay at least three. The ants are free. . .'

'Thanks,' we answered. 'Right now I don't need ants. I'm not from here, just a visitor.'

'Visitor?' the man's face lighted up. 'Just a sec!'

With that he disappeared into his station, coming back with about a dozen outsize maps which he spread all over the car.

'This car is somewhat neglected,' he remarked as he cleaned the car seats with a nylon brush. 'I have wonderful nylon brushes in all colours.'

'Thank you very much,' thus we, 'my uncle is in brushes.'

'You have an uncle here? Why not surprise him with a nice gift? I got real flower vases. Musical lamp shades. New! An accordion. Shaving soap. A parrot. . .'

'Thanks. I don't like my uncle all that much.'

'You are quite right, mister,' the attendant said and lightly vacuum cleaned my clothes. 'It's much better not to depend on one's relatives. I also deal in apartments. . .'

'Thanks, I'm on the road most of the time.'

'To which paper do you want to subscribe?'

'Thanks.'

'Learn to dance!'

'I can dance.'

'Oil shares?'

'I'm against that kind of thing.'

'OK. Two bucks.'

'What?'

'The ant farm.'

'I told you I don't need them now.'

'So what will you buy?' the attendant sighed and absent-mindedly combed my hair. I became somewhat nervous as I recalled that after all I had only come to buy gasoline. How was I going to get rid of this organizational genius?

'As a matter of fact,' I mused, 'I'm thinking of buying a concert piano. . .'

The attendant's face lighted up and he hurried over to his

store room. In a matter of seconds he was back with a sheaf of booklets in all the hues of the rainbow.

'For $1,200 I'll give you a German-made piano. I'll move it right into your apartment.'

That sounded interesting.

'All right,' I said, 'and what happens if you drop it on the stairs?'

'Nothing of the sort has ever happened to me,' the man assured me, 'but if you are afraid, for a supplement of $12 I'll write out an insurance policy for the wholeness of the instrument, because I happen to be the leading insurance agent in this area. Do you yourself play the piano?'

'No,' I answered, 'we always dreamt that our son would be a musician. . .'

'Fine,' the attendant beamed. 'For a monthly $18.50 I'll get you a graduate music teacher.'

'All right,' I mused, 'but what if the kid absolutely refuses to study?'

'$75 in three equal instalments,' thus he. 'For this little supplement I'll send you a famous child psychiatrist, who'll influence the brat in the right direction.'

'That sounds good,' I had to admit, 'the trouble is only that we have no kids. . .'

'For a one-time payment of $20 I'll send an expert to your place. . .'

Here I had a brainstorm:

'Just a second,' I interrupted the gas man. 'Do you also undertake the writing of travel books?'

'Of course. $1,500 for 100,000 printing marks.'

'But,' I said, 'it has to be funny.'

'That shouldn't be any problem. It's only $15 more per printing sheet. . .'

So this book was written by the station attendant whom I met on the way to New Haven. I put myself completely in his hands. Why bother?

Translated from the Hebrew by Yohanan Goldman

For those who like to sit down and watch or to fall asleep and be awakened when they arrive, we have a few selections on bus, train, and air travel. Although the industry's been having its problems, the bus still provides the most intensely American experience available. For some reason, people are more themselves on a bus than anywhere else—although often you wish they weren't—and it is on a bus that you most often find yourselves among locals who aren't traveling and may never travel at all, but who love to pull the legs of strangers, such as American travel writer Mary Day Winn.

Mary Day Winn
Camaraderie on a Bus   1931

THERE IS A SPIRIT OF CAMARADERIE on a bus such as one seldom finds on a train. The group of people in the little, self-contained unit are within sight and hearing of each other; all bump through the same mudhole at the same time, swallow the same cloud of dust from a passing car, look out simultaneously to thrill and exclaim over the same view. When the bus comes to a halt every two or three hours to make a rest stop in front of a roadside station, all get out to stretch their legs for a few minutes and to stand round the huge vehicle like a flock of chickens round a mother hen, smoking, gossiping, and munching chocolate bars.

Before we had reached Laramie, in the middle of the afternoon, we had talked to half the people on our coach, most of whom were natives of Wyoming or Colorado, and the land we were passing through had become a vivid background for the naive, the humorous, the heroic, or the picturesquely bad characters who had peopled this young country and were still writing its history in laughter and blood.

84

"They been having quite a celebration in Fairplay," said a bronzed farmer in overalls and a khaki jacket lined with sheep's wool; "a funeral celebration." He seemed to regard a funeral as quite an amusing affair. I must have looked my surprise. "Fairplay," he explained, "is a little town southwest of Denver. It and the town nearest have been contesting with each other as to which one would have the privilege of burying a noted citizen of the country."

"Which town did he live in?"

"He didn't exactly live in either. He'd stayed all his life, sixty-two years, under the ground, in a mine there."

"How horrible!"

"Yes, ma'am, it does sound so; but even at sixty-two he didn't die natural; they had to shoot him because he couldn't eat."

"Now," said Mr. Suydam, "you're spoofing us."

"No, sir. You didn't let me tell you that this citizen was a mule. . . . But mighty highly thought of in these parts. I don't know which town won out in the contest over his carcass, but I know they laid him away with a big ceremony and put up a monument over him." He was childishly delighted at our surprise.

⁑*The train is a more formal affair than a bus. Next, American writer William Saroyan tells a story about taking other people's advice about traveling by train.*

William Saroyan
To Heed or Not to Heed   1939

ONE YEAR MY UNCLE MELIK traveled from Fresno to New York. Before he got aboard the train his uncle Garro paid him a visit and told him about the dangers of travel.

When you get on the train, the old man said, choose your seat carefully, sit down, and do not look about.

Yes, sir, my uncle said.

Several moments after the train begins to move, the old man said, two men wearing uniforms will come down the aisle and ask you for your ticket. Ignore them. They will be imposters.

How will I know? my uncle said.

You will know, the old man said. You are no longer a child.

Yes, sir, my uncle said.

Before you have traveled twenty miles an amiable young man will come to you and offer you a cigarette. Tell him you don't smoke. The cigarette will be doped.

Yes, sir, said my uncle.

On your way to the diner a very beautiful young woman will bump into you intentionally and almost embrace you, the old man said. She will be extremely apologetic and attractive, and your natural impulse will be to cultivate her friendship. Dismiss your natural impulse and go on in and eat. The woman will be an adventuress.

A what? my uncle said.

A whore, the old man shouted. Go on in and eat. Order the best food, and if the diner is crowded, and the beautiful young woman sits across the table from you, do not look into her eyes. If she speaks, pretend to be deaf.

Yes, sir, my uncle said.

Pretend to be deaf, the old man said. That is the only way out of it.

Out of what? my uncle said.

Out of the whole ungodly mess, the old man said. I have traveled. I know what I'm talking about.

Yes, sir, my uncle said.

Let's say no more about it, the old man said.

Yes, sir, my uncle said.

Let's not speak of the matter again, the old man said. It's finished. I have seven children. My life has been a full and righteous one. Let's not give it another thought. I have land, vines, trees, cattle, and money. One cannot have everything—except for a day or two at a time.

Yes, sir, my uncle said.

On your way back to your seat from the diner, the old man said, you will pass through the smoker. There you will find a game of cards in progress. The players will be three middle-aged men with expensive-looking rings on their fingers. They will nod at you pleasantly and one of them will invite you to join the game. Tell them, No speak English.

Yes, sir, my uncle said.

That is all, the old man said.

Thank you very much, my uncle said.

One thing more, the old man said. When you go to bed at night, take your money out of your pocket and put it in your shoe. Put your shoe under your pillow, keep your head on the pillow all night, *and don't sleep*.

Yes, sir, my uncle said.

That is all, the old man said.

The old man went away and the next day my uncle Melik got aboard the train and traveled straight across America to New York. The two men in uniforms were not imposters, the young man with the doped cigarette did not arrive, the beautiful young woman did not sit across the table from my uncle in the diner, and there was no card game in progress in the smoker. My uncle put his money in his shoe and put his shoe under his pillow and put his head on the pillow and didn't sleep all night the first night, but the second night he abandoned the whole ritual.

The second day he *himself* offered another young man a cigarette which the other young man accepted. In the diner my uncle went out of his way to sit at a table with a young lady. He started a poker game in the smoker, and long before the train ever got to New York my uncle knew everybody aboard the train and everybody knew him. Once, while the train was traveling through Ohio, my uncle and the young man who had accepted the cigarette and two young ladies on their way to Vassar formed a quartette and sang *The Wabash Blues*.

The journey was a very pleasant one.

When my uncle Melik came back from New York, his old uncle Garro visited him again.

I see you are looking all right, he said. Did you follow my instructions?

Yes, sir, my uncle said.

The old man looked far away in space.

I am pleased that *someone* has profited by my experience, he said.

Flying is certainly the most efficient, if not the most personal, way to travel from one part of the U.S. to another. For foreigners, who have much less reason to fly than we do, long-distance flying is an experience in itself, as British novelist William Golding, best known here for his novel Lord of the Flies, *shows us in his selection on flying cross-country, body and soul.*

William Golding
Body and Soul   1965

EAST COAST BLANKED OUT from North Carolina right up to the Canadian border; a half-continent under a pat of fog; nothing visible but the extreme tip of the Empire State Building; planes grounded. Fog, the airman's common cold; all the resources of science are squeaking and gibbering under it; lights blink unseen, radar echoes quiver and ping; the gigantic aircraft lumber round the ramps and aprons like death's-head moths in cold weather; money leaks away. We, the privileged, sit in a sort of underground air-raid shelter, racked by public-address systems and blasts of furious air-conditioning. Evening drags into night. Everything is astonishingly dirty, and time itself is stale. We sit.

Most passengers drift away, to go by train, or try a night's sleep in the airport hotel. But I am going too far to get there any way but by jet. Tomorrow I give the first of three lectures in Los Angeles, on the other side of America. Here it is midnight, or past midnight, or feels like midnight. I am late already, and must go by what flight I can. I cannot telegraph anyone, even though I shall land at the wrong airport.

A loudspeaker honks and burbles. Incredibly, and for the next hour, we have take-off and landing limits. Our plane is getting through; and sure enough, presently it bumbles out of the fog from the runway. I go with our group to Gate Nine, shudder into a freezing night with a dull grey roof. The jet crawls towards us, howling and whistling with rage, perhaps at the fog or perhaps at the human bondage which keeps it only just under control. For a moment or two, it faces us—no, is end-on to us; for here there is no touch of human, or animal, or insect, no face—only four holes that scream like nothing else in creation. Then it huddles round and is still. Doors open and two streams of passengers ooze out. Their faces are haggard. They ignore the night that has caught up with them. They stagger, or walk with the stiff gait of stage sleep-walkers. One or two look stunned, as if they know it is midnight more or less but cannot remember if it is today or tomorrow midnight and why or what. Strange vehicles flashing all over with red lights come out of the darkness, not for the passengers, but to tend the jet. They crouch under the wings and the front end, attach themselves by tubes while all their lights flash, and lights on the jet flash, and the engines sink from a wail to a moan—a note, one might think, of resignation, as if the machine now recognizes that it is caught and will have to do the whole thing over again. But for half an hour they feed it well, while it sucks or they blow, and we stand, imprisoned by the freezing cold and our own need to be somewhere else. Jet travel is a great convenience.

Then we are in, fastening safety belts, and I peer out of the window with a naivete which seems to increase as I grow older; and a succession of blue lights flick by faster and faster; and there is an eternity of acceleration at an angle of forty-five degrees, while the whistling holes under the wings seem no longer angry but godlike—see what we can do! Look, no hands! The 'No Smoking, Fasten Your Safety Belts' notice disappears. Cupping my hands round my face, squinting sideways and down, I can make out that there is a white pat of fog slipping by beneath us, and over it a few stationary stars. An air hostess demonstrates the use of the oxygen masks.

Comfort, warmth flowing back into rigid hands, comparative silence, stillness except for an occasional nudge as the plane pierces a furlong of turbulence; I try to think of what our airspeed means: it remains nothing but arithmetic. The interior of the plane is like a very superior bus. Am thawed and relaxed. They say that this is not the latest mark of jet—do jets come any faster or bigger or plusher?

Glasses tinkle. Air Hostess brings round drinks—not what happens in a bus. Select Bourbon. (Always live off the country as far as possible.) I also secrete the TWA swizzle-stick as a memento. Do not cross America often this way. Another Bourbon. That makes the two obligatory drinks before an American dinner. Am cheerful now—but second drink did not contain swizzlestick and wonder if I am detected? Air Hostess approaches for the third time and I cower—but no. She is English and recognizes a fellow-countryman. Speaks Kensingtonian, which sounds odd at this place and altitude. (Note to intending immigrants. Kensingtonian despised in a man. Gets him called a pouf. Do not know exactly what this terms means, but cannot think it complimentary. On the other hand, Kensingtonian in a girl widely approved of, Americans think it cute.)

Peripeteia! English Air Hostess has read my books and seen me on English telly! I instantly acquire overwhelming status. Feel utterly happy and distinguished in a nice, diffident, English sort of way. Neighbour puts away his briefcase—we all have briefcases—then talks to me. Is physicist, naturally. Tells me about jets sucking air in at one end and blowing result of combustion out at the other. Encourage him, from a pure sense of *joie de vivre*. Rash, this, very. Tells me about navigation lights, navigation, fluids, including the sea, acceleration—Bourbon now dying down. Make my way forward to lavatory in diffident but distinguished manner, watched by all the unhappy briefcases who haven't been on telly, or haven't been noticed there by an Air Hostess. Lavatory wonderful, buttons everywhere. Push the lot, just to tell grandchildren. Tiny, ultimate fraction of our airstream is scooped in somewhere and directed to blow a jet vertically up out of the pan. Could balance celluloid balls on it and shoot them down with a rifle, as at fairs.

Return to seat and physicist continues course. American Air Hostess comes and talks. More status. Physicist goes to sleep. English Air Hostess comes and talks about London, Paris, Rome, Athens. American Air Hostess counters with Hawaii and Japan. Slight loss of status. I would like to go to sleep. Body here, can see it sitting in the seat. Soul still

1)

2.)

3.)

Anatol Kovarsky. By permission of the artist.

sunny Los Angeles and up the Del Monica heights where the fire was. Body sees mountain road of burnt houses for film stars. Only thing left is row of swimming pools built on stilts out over the gorge, since there is nowhere else for them.

Descent to Pacific. Waves coming the wrong way—no, that was the Atlantic. Sherry in house. Lunch in university. Forty thousand students, or is it seventy? Own campus police and bus service. After lunch, body looks at lecture notes, but cannot bring itself to care. Body gives first lecture and hears its mouth making the appropriate noises. Soul not really necessary in this game. Has drinks beneath original Beerbohm cartoons. Has dinner with the Christmas Story lining the road outside, each tableau the size of a cottage with full-size figures in plaster and floodlit. Party after dinner. Body is told about the definitive Dickens and the Boswell factory. Body is nearly frightened to hear itself advise against the export of American novels. Stick to cars, it says. Soul would be very angry if it could hear that. Body finds itself getting smaller, or is it larger? Is led away, and falls on English-type bed with knobs at each corner.

At two o'clock in the morning there seemed to be a second person present. With the sort of effort one makes to achieve binocular vision, they united themselves; and soul in body, I was looking at the ceiling of a hotel bedroom in Los Angeles. The luxury of being whole was such that I could not sleep, but smoked till I felt like stockfish. The real trouble was that I had a defect of imagination which would not let me believe I was where I was, and yet I knew I was in Los Angeles. Being whole, I was immediately frightened at the vision of tomorrow's lecture and began to compose it in my sleepless head. That way the day dawned, and just as I ran out of cigarettes, my nice bearleader telephoned to set up the morning's sightseeing. We saw the Mormon temple, with a gold angel on the tower, far larger than any God has in heaven. We saw the colossal Medical Centre where the corridors run clean out of perspective to infinity at a point; where the patient is taken in at one end and can be served

94

up as a complete set of demonstration slides at the other. We saw the beach—and for a moment I was really where I was—watching the waves turn over, and stunned by the acute realization that this had been here all the time, had not been created in Europe and exported to form part of a set. I lectured again, pleaded for an evening in bed, but sneaked off on my own—*peccavi*—and had dinner; filet mignon and a bottle of burgundy-type wine. (Note for wines-men: it was an Almaden '57; suffered like all California wines from that fatal inferiority complex—but once convinced you were a friend, it would offer you what it had.) At two in the morning carried my filet mignon and my burgundy-type wine back to my English-type bed, and lay with my head full of tomorrow's lecture. Dawn.

Nice bearleader came and took me to see the San Gabriel mountains with snow on them and the Chinese Theatre, its pavements with footprints, handprints, graffiti of film stars on them; showed me Hollywood, Gangster's Corner, Mae West's hotel, the William Andrews Clarke Memorial Library. For ten ridiculously exciting seconds I held the MS of *The Importance of Being Earnest* in my hands. (You, too, have been awarded an Oscar!) We finished that jaunt in a bowling alley, where the beer was good, the telly in colour and the machines for setting up the pins seemed, in their implacable devotion, to be much more intelligent than anything else in sight.

I lecture, meet students, and pack grip in a flash. Meet faculty. Party. Nth, I think. Now I am taken to dinner in an English-type restaurant to make me feel at home. Recognize it as English instantly, because the bartender and all the waiters are in full hunting kit. At one moment they gather round a table and sing 'Happy Birthday' in close harmony. Los Angeles is the mostest, am utterly happy. What other place et cetera. Am eating abalone, the local must, and talking in six directions at once, but am suddenly seized and rushed away to jet, leaving soul still continuing conversations. Body loses way down to plane and is nearly sucked through engine, ha ha. Acceleration and fifty miles *square* of lights tilts under us. This is the latest mark of jet, they say, can see no difference, that is the Pacific down there, time, eleven o'clock.

American Air Hostess brings round Bourbon. Secrete swizzlestick. Another Bourbon. American Southern Belle-type Air Hostess, v. pretty, guesses I am English and a writer (beard in jet), comes and sits! Immense status SBAH did Creative Writing Course at College. Said to her Prof.: 'Ah aim to be a writer.' Prof. said: 'What do you know about life?' SBAH said: 'Ah hev written a critical essay on Thomas Wolfe and a short story which ah would like you to read.' Prof. read story, said: 'Go and be an Air Hostess'—'So heah ah em!' Delightful girl, there ought to be a lot more of them and there probably are. Supper. Go to lavatory and discover this really *is* the latest mark of jet. Tiny, ultimate fraction of our airstream is scooped in somewhere, let into the pan and merely chases itself round and round and round.

Am tucked up solicitously for the night, but am still able to see out of the window, my goodness me, no sleep with a view like that. America sliding by, 650 miles an hour airspeed with 150 miles an hour tail wind; 800 miles an hour over the ground—no cloud. Cities, gleaming, glowing ravishments slide under us six miles down, lines of phosphorescence scored at right-angles to each other. Moon and snow. Stars, perceptibly wheeling. More molten cities. Body understands that America is crust of earth with fire inside, must break out somewhere, hence these scores, these right-angled lava cracks, these chessboard patterns of luminosity (with here and there a wink of veritable incandescence like the white spark on a red coal), but all soft as the tiny lights of a shock cradle. Garish street lamps, Christmas Decorations, traffic signals, window displays, sky signs, now softened, softened. Body lines up jet-hole with city—sees it swallow a whole street six miles long in seconds, how to take the children to school, scoop! three blocks of run-down houses, park, Motel, Motel, Motel, parking lot, cemetery, jump the sparking traffic lights, scoop! Drugstore, Charlies Cheeseburgers, Eats, Frolic Fashion House, Beautician, Physician, Mortician, Realty, News Office WinnDixieMountjoyToyTownSurplusWarStockCrossroads ChurchofChrist(Airconditioning)Square!MayoraltyFireStation PoliceStationHowardJohnsonSquare!LightsLightsLightsSquare! LightsLightsLightsRiverSquare! All sucked in and blown out, scooped up, hurled back, august, imperial, god-like, America, oh from up here and at this power, even unto weeping, America The——

SBAH is tinkling glasses and switching on lights. My God. Breakfast! Four hours out from Los Angeles—where soul is still engaged in fierce discussion of freedom, birth control, how to be happy though British, Emblems—four hours out, there is ahead of us the distinction between grey and black that betokens dawn over the curved Atlantic. Sure enough, the sweeper is switched off for a thirty-minutes' descent. Poor soul, no longer the centre of my sinful earth, but setting out just now on that long climb over the Rockies. Fasten your safety belts. And the time is. . . .

it wasn't a Madison Avenue technique.

Eric Sloane

NOVA BRITANNIA.

OFFRING MOST

Excellent fruites by Planting in
VIRGINIA.

Exciting all such as be well affected
to further the same.

LONDON
Printed for SAMVEL MACHAM, and are to be sold at
his Shop in Pauls Church-yard, at the
Signe of the Bul-head.
1 6 0 9.

Title page of first American tourist pamphlet, 1609.

A TOUR OF THE REPUBLIC

❧Introduction

❧*Okay, now we're ready to fasten our seat belts, shift into high gear, and get a move on. But before we visit any actual part of the country, we'll take a look at that most popular subject of conversation in the universe and the thing that above all else determines how our vacation goes: the weather. And who can better share with us the extremes of American weather than the man of all seasons and all (American) places, Charles Kuralt, with the most accurate—or, at least, the most enjoyable—descriptions of American weather he has picked up in his years of interviewing ordinarily extraordinary Americans.*

Charles Kuralt
American Weather 1985

WELL, THE SUN WAS SHINING a few minutes ago, but now it looks like there's a big storm coming. Mark Twain, remarking on American weather, said one time that he sat in one place and counted 136 different kinds of weather inside of twenty-four hours. That may be an exaggeration. When it comes to the weather, Americans do tend to exaggerate. So, when we decided to do a national weather survey, we sought out only exceptionally truthful individuals like my friend Roger Welsch, a Nebraska tree farmer and keen observer of Nebraska weather.

KURALT: When the real dog days come, it does get hot in Nebraska.

ROGER WELSCH: I don't think there's any place hotter than Nebraska in the summer. Down here by the river, just not too far from us, it'll get so dry that the catfish will come up here to the house and get a drink at the pump. Yep, really. Yeah. And a lot of the farmers around here will feed their chickens cracked ice so they won't lay hard-boiled eggs.

Well you may laugh, but the hot weather leads to tragedy sometimes. Kendall Morse remembers what happened in Maine.

KENDALL MORSE: Oh, it was so hot here in Maine last summer that one day—it was right in the middle of corn season, that corn was almost ripe—and it got so hot that the corn started to pop, and it popped and it went all over the place. And there was a herd of cows right next to that cornfield and they looked up and they saw that popcorn coming down like that. And cows are not very bright, of course. They thought it was snow. And every one of them idiot cows stood there and froze to death!

For Maine, of course, that was a hot day. Here's a Hoosier weather report from Charles Porter.

CHARLES PORTER: It was so hot here one day in Odon, Indiana, you could take a frozen hamburger patty out of the freezer, toss it up in the air, and when it came down it was cooked well done. But you had to be careful and not toss it up too high. If you did, it came back down burned.

We went to Arizona in midsummer to ask Jim Griffith how he and his neighbors are holding up.

JIM GRIFFITH: It does get a little bit warm. Joe Harris says it usually gets so hot and dry in the summertime that he's got to prime himself before he can spit. And the dog's sort of wandering around at midnight trying to find some shade to lay down in. It does warm up a little bit, but you get used to it. It's been known, especially in this part of Arizona, to get so dry that the trees will follow the dogs around.

That's dry, all right. But right there in Nebraska, Roger

Welsch's wife has to run their well through a wringer this time of year to get enough water to cook with. And the river gets low, of course.

WELSCH: They talk about frogs that would grow up to be three and four years old without ever having learned how to swim. And they'd have to, in the schools, you know, get little cans and put holes in the bottom and sprinkle water so that kids could see what it was and wouldn't panic the first time they saw it rain. They tell about one farmer who's out plowing one day and it started to rain, and the first drops that hit him shocked him so that he passed out. And to bring him to, they had to throw two buckets of dust in his face!

Oh, it's been a dry summer, but it sure was a wet spring. Don Reed remembers how wet it got in the Middle West.

DON REED: In Minnesota, the floods were so bad that the turtles crawled out of their shells and used the shells as rowboats.

PORTER: the raindrops were so big here one day, it only took one raindrop to fill a quart jar.

Big as those Indiana raindrops were, they weren't as big as some Ed Bell remembers from a Texas storm back in '73.

ED BELL: There was one place there that I noticed raindrops nearly as big as a number-three washtub and they formed a kind of marching pattern coming straight down, one right behind the other, and it wore a hole in the ground that we used for a well. And ten years later, we are still drawing rainwater out of that well.

What rain they get in the Great Plains comes all at once, eight or ten inches in one day and that's it for the year. Every farmer has a little lane out to the highway and the rains on the plains fall mainly on the lanes.

WELSCH: Like this road of mine, there's some holes out here you can run set lines in and catch fish out of the road. And there's one farmer who talked about finally having to walk into town, because his wagon wouldn't get up his lane. So, he had to walk into town to get some groceries, and he found this huge puddle out in the middle of his road.

And there was a nice hat floating around in the center. So, he reached out with his foot and kicked in this hat, and there was a guy's head under it. So, he got down on his hands and knees and he said, "Are you all right, stranger?" And the guy said, "Well I guess so, I'm on horseback."

Wherever you got puddles like that, of course, you get mosquitos. I thought we had big mosquitos back home in North Carolina. My grandfather told me he saw a couple once the size of crows, and heard 'em talking about him. One of those mosquitos said, "Shall we eat him here or take him with us?" The other one said, "Well, we better eat him here. If we take him with us, the big guys will take him away from us." What surprised me was to learn that they grow mosquitos bigger than that out West.

JIM GRIFFITH: They get reasonably good-sized, not so big that you can't shoot 'em down with a scattergun. You know, you don't have to take a rifle to 'em, but they get pretty good-sized. But the really big ones are up in southern Nevada. There was one, I remember, it was in the papers at the time, there was one that come in to Nellis Air Force Base up there, and they filled it up with high-octane fuel before they realized that it had the wrong markings on it. And—

KURALT: That was a big mosquito.

GRIFFITH: That was a good-sized mosquito, yeah. That was pretty good-sized.

I should mention again I'm not sure all these stories are true. Americans do lie sometimes. There was a fellow down home with such a reputation for lying that he had to have a neighbor come in to call his hogs. But if these aren't true stories, they're about as true as any other weather reports you're likely to hear.

In the middle of August, it's easy to forget how cold it was last winter. A friend of mine who lives in a cabin in Montana told me it was so cold there that the flame froze on his candle and he had to take it outside and bury it to get it dark enough to sleep. Sidney Boyum says it was cold in Wisconsin, too.

SIDNEY BOYUM: It was so cold here in Madison that a night

crawler came out of the ground, mugged a caterpillar, stole his fur coat, and went back into the ground.

You know it's cold when you see something like that happen. In Maine, Joe Perham says it was an awful quiet winter.

JOE PERHAM: Well, it was so cold last winter up here in Maine that the words froze right in our mouths. That's right. We had to wait till spring to find out what we'd been talking about all winter.

The real old-timers remember a winter like that in Nebraska. They still talk about the blizzard of '88.

WELSCH: The worst part was the first day of spring, 'cause you couldn't hear yourself think, for all the rooster crows and train whistles that were thawing out. Another guy said, no, the worst part was milking, because he said it was so cold that when you milked, the milk would freeze before it hit the bottom of the bucket; and another guy said, well, they learned how to deal with that in their family. They'd milk with one arm out. They'd milk out over their arm until they had an armload of frozen squirts. And they'd tie that up with binder twine and put it up in the barn till their mother was cooking and she'd send them out for however many squirts the recipe called for.

Arizonans are not much troubled by cold weather, of course. But that desert is about the windiest place I've ever been.

KURALT *[as gusts blow the sand]:* Does the wind always blow this way?

GRIFFITH: Well, no, Charles. About half the time it backs around and blows the other way. In the summertime, the west wind blows so darn hard that it causes the sun to set three hours later than it does in the wintertime.

KURALT *[to Welsch]:* I guess the wind blows here in Nebraska sometimes, huh?

WELSCH: All the time. They say one day the wind stopped and everybody fell down.

Ed Bell says they had a pretty good windstorm in Texas just this spring.

BELL: Folks, that was a wind! The wind blew and blew and blew. It just got harder and harder; blew the bark off the trees, blew all the feathers off of chickens, even blew the four tires off the old Model-T Ford; turned a bulldog wrong side out.

REED: A fellow in northern Wisconsin wrote that in 1976 they had a windstorm so bad that it stretched his telephone wires so far that when he called his neighbor across the street, he was billed $17.60 plus tax for long distance telephone charges.

PORTER: I was out in the front yard one day and we had a windstorm came through there. That wind was so strong, it blew a big iron kettle across the front yard so fast, the lightning had to strike it five times before it got a hit.

WELSCH: Easterners often notice that in Nebraska, unlike other parts of the country, there aren't wind vanes on the barns, 'cause what you normally do is look out and see which way the barn is leaning, and that will tell you which way the wind's blowing. But they do have a Nebraska wind directional teller, which is a post in the ground with a logging chain on the end, and then you just watch to see which way the logging chain blows to tell which way the wind's from. And you can tell the wind speed by how many links are being snapped off at the end.

Well, of course, you'd expect the wind to blow hard in Nebraska, because there's nothing between there and the North Pole but a couple of barbed wire fences. And if somebody leaves one of the gates open, then there's nothing to stop the wind, all the way down.

PERHAM: Wind? Well, the wind blew so hard here last night that the hen laid the same egg four times.

Laid the same egg four times. That was in Maine. This is Chuck Larkin, who lives in Georgia.

CHUCK LARKIN: I seen a chicken, just this afternoon, standing with her back to the wind, laid the same egg five times.

Five times in Georgia!

WELSCH: The other day someone told me that they had a chicken here that laid the same egg seven times.

Seven times in Nebraska!

GRIFFITH: Old Joe was raising chickens and first thing that happened was that he got 'em back the wrong way in the wind, and the old hen laid the same egg fourteen times over before she finally got it out.

Fourteen times in Arizona! I told you Arizona was the windiest place of all! But then, it's a pretty windy country, as you may have noticed.

Manfred Hausmann. By permission of S. Fischer Verlag GMBH, Frankfurt am Main.

❧New York

❧*New York, New York is just that. Nothing more and nothing less. In our east-leaning history of European tourists and immigrants, it was the first stop for most, and for many the last stop as well.*

People go to New York for many reasons: to get away from someplace small or to make it big; to live something down or to live it up. Some people even go there on business. Whatever the reason, New York is a powerful magnet which attracts as many people as it repels. It is a city of extremes, stretching from New York all the way to New York.

No one could make New York City up, yet some writers aren't satisfied with it. They still insist on using it as a diving board to greater (or lesser) fantasies. Take our first, parodic selection by British novelist William Makepeace Thackeray. And in the second selection, Crosbie Garstin discovers both the fantasy and the reality of New York.

W. M. Thackeray
An Imaginary Letter from
New York 1848

DEAR MADAM:—
It seems to me a long time since I had the honour of seeing you. I shall be glad to have some account of your health. We made a beautiful voyage of 13 1/2 days, and reached this fine city yesterday. The entrance of the bay is beautiful; magnificent woods of the Susquehannah stretch down to the shore, and from Hoboken lighthouse to

Vancouver's Island, the bay presents one brilliant blaze of natural and commercial loveliness. Hearing that Titmarsh was on board the steamer, the Lord Mayor and Alderman of New York came down to receive us, and the batteries on Long Island fired a salute. General Jackson called at my hotel, (the Astor house). I found him a kind old man, though he has a wooden leg and takes a great deal of snuff. Broadway has certainly disappointed me—it is nothing to be compared to our own dear Holborn Hill. But the beautiful range of the Allegheney mountains, which I see from my windows, and the roar of the Niagara Cataract, which empties itself out of the Mississippi into the Oregon territory, have an effect, which your fine eye for the picturesque, and keen sense of the beautiful and the natural would I am sure lead you to appreciate.

The oysters here are much larger than ours, and the canvass backed ducks, are reckoned, and indeed are, a delicacy. The house where Washington was born is still shown, but the General I am informed, is dead, much regretted. The clergy here is both numerous and respected, and the Archbishop of New York is a most venerable and delightful prelate; whose sermons are however a little long.

· ·

Your very faithful servt.,

W. M. Thackeray

Crosbie Garstin
Fantasy or Not? 1927

NEW YORK IS NOT A REAL CITY, it's a fantasy in ferro-concrete. When I first approached the place it was on a frosty midwinter evening. We had sloppy weather throughout the voyage and the old *St. Louis* nosed past Robbins Reef and Bedloe's Isle, her decks slippery with ice. Black velvet night had blotted out the buildings and left nothing but lights. The myriad windows of the downtown skyscrapers were lit up and had the appearance of strings of fiery tinsel suspended from heaven. Great electric skysigns glowed over Broadway, white, ruby, emerald, leaping, fading and leaping again. Illuminated ferry boats slid across the invisible Hudson, looking like ambulant glass houses ablaze within. The railway depots on the Jersey side were crowned with huge letters of fire. The sight took my breath away. This was not the hustling, bustling, clanging, ultra-modern metropolis I had expected, but a dream-city blazing like some barbaric queen in living jewels, an immense fantasy in fairy lights.

When I approached New York for the second time it fell as flat as a sand-dab. The reason was the time of day. It takes natures more soulful than mine to become really enthusiastic at seven in the morning, especially if, thanks to a somewhat protracted farewell party, one has only reached one's bed at six. We crawled through the grey of morning towards the White Star dock, the little tugs nosing round us like suckling pigs at a sow. There were no festoons and necklaces and coronets of coloured lights winking and glittering in the black velvet night. No fantasy, no magic. I told my disgruntled self that New York was real, after all. Those looming grey cliffs were just skyscrapers; everything here was just like everything elsewhere, only a bit taller. There was nothing in it. Washout!

With Canadian novelist Robertson Davies' observations as sandwich meat, two of America's best-known humorous columnists, Art Buchwald and Russell Baker, tell, respectively, how New York got its bad name and how the anxieties that make up the essence of New York appear to a visitor from Iowa.

Art Buchwald
I Love New York 1983

NEW YORKERS ARE ALWAYS COMPLAINING that "foreigners" (those who don't live there) are giving the city a bad name. Actually, we "foreigners" would have no idea what was going on unless New Yorkers told us.

I had occasion to visit New York on a Sunday recently, and spent the afternoon in Queens at a gathering of friends. Then I announced that I had to go into the city.

"How are you planning to go?" someone asked.

"I thought I'd take the subway," I replied.

"You can't take the subway!" the person said.

"Why? It's Sunday. The subway shouldn't be too crowded."

"That's just the point," another friend told me. "It's much more dangerous to take it when it isn't crowded. You could be sitting in a car all by yourself, and that's when they'll get you."

"If they don't get you, the subway will," another person said.

"How could the subway get me?" I wanted to know.

"It's always breaking down. You could be stuck under the East River all night long."

"Maybe I'd better take a taxi."

"Be careful. Don't tell the cab driver you're from out of

109

town, or he'll take you to Manhattan via Staten Island. They wait all day for people like you."

Another friend said, "If he does take you by way of Staten Island, don't argue with him. There was a story in the newspaper the other day about a man who complained the taxi was taking the long way from Kennedy Airport, and the driver beat him up with a tire iron."

"How long are you staying in Manhattan?" someone inquired.

"Just a couple of days."

"I'd take off that watch if I were you. They're getting awfully good at ripping off watches. If your wife is going to be with you, tell her not to wear any gold chains. They'll rip them off, too."

"Where are you staying?"

"Down in Gramercy Park," I said.

"You weren't planning on going out at night, were you?"

"I was hoping to. I understand there's a lot to see in New York City at night."

Someone said, "It depends on where you go. Always walk on a lighted street near the curb, and if they ask for your money, give it to them without arguing."

"Better still, don't walk anywhere. Take a taxi, and tell the driver to wait until you get into the hotel lobby," a friend added.

"It is all right to go to the theater?" I asked.

"It's all right to go. But coming back is when you could get into trouble. Whatever you do, stay off Eighth Avenue. That's where all the crazies hang out."

"Before you go, put all your valuables in the hotel safe, and be sure when you get back to your hotel to double-lock your door. I know a guy who was sleeping in one of the best hotels in the city and found someone going through his trousers looking for his wallet."

"I think I better take notes," I said. "I hear the restaurants are pretty good in New York."

"It depends if they know you or not. If you go to one of

the better ones, make sure you slip the headwaiter a twenty-dollar bill, or you'll be standing at the bar until eleven o'clock at night."

"When you're leaving for the airport during the rush hour, give yourself two hours. If one car breaks down on the East Side Drive, you're a dead duck."

"Gosh," I said. "This sounds like a tough city."

"Why do you say that?" someone asked defensively.

"No reason," I replied, realizing I was on dangerous ground.

"That's the trouble with you out-of-towners. You're always knocking New York because you don't live here. It's the greatest place in the world."

"I better get going," I said.

"Why? It's only four o'clock."

"Well, if I'm going to get beaten up with a tire iron, I better allow some time to go to the hospital."

"If you go to the emergency room on Sunday," a friend said, "make sure there's an English-speaking doctor on duty."

Robertson Davies
Show Me to Your Con Men 1947

HAVING HEARD MANY TRAVELLERS' TALES of the dreadful deceptions practised upon strangers in New York, I walked about the city today expecting to be accosted by men who wanted to sell me gold bricks, or possibly the controlling interest in Brooklyn Bridge. However, nothing of the sort happened. Decided that perhaps my appearance was too urbane, so this afternoon I tried chewing a straw and saying, "Wal I swan to thunderation!" every time I looked at a high building. Still no rush of confidence men. Perhaps the perils of New York are exaggerated. . . .

Russell Baker
The New York Experience 1980

OUR FRIEND WINOKUR, who is ill at ease in New York, arrived from Iowa for a visit recently and immediately noticed two cucumbers on the sidewalk in front of our house. Apparently he had never seen cucumbers on a sidewalk before.

"Should I bring in these cucumbers?" he asked. We all smiled at his rustic simplicity and advised him to let sidewalk cucumbers lie. "Why are there cucumbers in front of your house?" he asked.

Nobody tried to answer that. We are New Yorkers. In New York different things turn up lying in front of your house. Sometimes they are cucumbers. Who knows why? Who cares? "This is New York, Winokur," I said. "Enjoy it, and don't get bogged down in cucumbers."

We gave him a potion to calm his anxiety and bedded him down on the first floor. Having stayed with us in the past, he refuses to sleep upstairs for fear of being crushed by objects falling off the Emperor, the forty-six-story apartment building across the street. The last time he visited, the Emperor shed an entire window of thick plate glass and crushed a car in front of our house. We assured him that the Emperor was always doing that sort of thing, that nobody had been killed yet and that when somebody was, the police would do something about it, since this was the high-rent district and in New York the upper-income folks got action from the law.

Winokur was not reassured. In Iowa, I gather, they don't have buildings that litter. He insisted on the downstairs sofa, but we had scarcely snuggled down for the night when he was upstairs rapping at the bedroom door.

"It sounds like somebody's stealing hubcaps out front," he said. Why did he think law-abiding New Yorkers went to bed at night, if not to allow hubcap thieves the right to work in privacy? Winokur was unhappy with this explanation. "Why don't you go to the window and look?" he suggested.

He was clearly uneasy about going to the window himself, and sensibly so, since you can never tell when the Emperor will send some plate glass sailing out from the thirty-fifth floor, across the street and right into the window where you are investigating a hubcap theft.

So I went to the window. Sure enough, a man was removing the rear hubcaps from a red sedan parked under the Emperor. He was a short, elegantly dressed man with a mustache, and his work was being admired by a large, heavy, well-dressed woman, obviously his wife or companion. I described all this to Winokur.

"Why is a well-dressed man removing hubcaps at midnight?" he asked. "Why is a well-dressed woman watching?"

"Why are there two cucumbers lying on the sidewalk in front of my house?" I explained.

Dissatisfied, Winokur came to the window. "The elegantly dressed man is now putting both hubcaps on the wall at the base of the Emperor," he whispered. "And now, he and the well-dressed stout woman are walking away."

"This is New York," I said.

"Somebody is going to come along and see those hubcaps and take them," said Winokur.

"Not necessarily," I said. "One night when I parked my car out there somebody came along, lifted the hood, stole the radiator hose and didn't even touch the hubcaps."

"Something very funny is going on here," said Winokur. "Fancy-dress couple take off hubcaps. Leave hubcaps where they're sure to be stolen. Obviously, they don't need the hubcaps, they don't want the hubcaps, they just want the hubcaps to be stolen."

Predictably enough, the loose hubcaps were spotted by two very civilized-looking men who seemed to be out for a stroll. They stopped, discussed the hubcaps and, picking them up, walked away with them, one hubcap per stroller. They didn't look like men who really needed hubcaps.

Winokur's Midwestern sense of decency was so offended that he threw up the window and shouted, "Put those hubcaps down." They didn't, of course. Winokur was baffled by this example of white-collar street crime, which was not at all mysterious to a New Yorker.

The man who removed the hubcaps, I explained, hated the owner of the red sedan for having a free parking place at the curb while he had none. In fact, he regarded that curb space as his very own and had taken vengeance, possibly at his wife's urging, by promoting the theft of his enemy's hubcaps.

"Ridiculous," said Winokur.

"This is New York," I said.

I sent him out for the papers next morning. "Somebody has stolen the cucumbers," he said, returning, "and now there's a slice of pizza lying where the cucumbers were yesterday." Life must be very strange in Iowa.

🕭To many, the essence of New York is its buildings. New York is the only city where an architecture critic can have as much influence as a political cartoonist. Here is the Russian poet Vladimir Mayakovsky, viewing New York's mountainous architecture through the binoculars of the Russian Revolution and revolutionary futurism.

Vladimir Mayakovsky
New York Is Not Modern 1925

THE INDUSTRIAL AGE, this is what Mayakovsky arrived in New York a few days ago to see, Mayakovsky, who for the past ten years has been the best-known poet in Soviet Russia, the voice of its new storm and chaos and construction, the laureate of its new machinery, the apostle of industrialism to a nation still half Asiatic and medieval.

"No, New York is not modern," he said, in his room near Washington Square, as he restlessly paced the floor. "New York is unorganized. Mere machinery, subways, skyscrapers and the like do not make a real industrial civilization. These are only the externals.

"America has gone through a tremendous material development which has changed the face of the world. But the people have not yet caught up to their new world . . . Intellectually, New Yorkers are still provincials. Their minds have not accepted the full implications of the industrial age.

"That is why I say New York is unorganized—it is a gigantic accident stumbled upon by children, not the full-grown, mature product of men who understood what they wanted and planned it like artists. When our industrial age comes to Russia it will be different—it will be planned—it will be conscious. . .

"Or take these self-same skyscrapers of yours. They are glorious achievements of the modern engineer. The past knew nothing like them. The plodding hand-workers of the Renaissance never dreamed of these great structures that sway in the wind and defy the laws of gravity. Fifty stories upward they march into the sky; and they should be clean, swift, complete, and modern as a dynamo. But the American builder, only half-aware of the miracle he has produced, scatters obsolete and silly Gothic and Byzantine ornaments over the skyscrapers. It is like tying pink ribbons on a steam dredge, or like putting Kewpie figures on a locomotive. . .

And now for a look at the action in New York. After all, what would New York be without action? No, not holdups and police chases. I'm referring to Society, about which we have a few comments by none other than a Rothschild, and every New Yorker's favorite sport, crossing the street, the rules and strategies of which will be explained by Sig Spaeth.

To finish off this section, classic American humorist Will Rogers takes only a few words to show the relationship between New Yorkers and visitors to New York.

Salomon de Rothschild
Unjust 1861

I MUST CONFESS that New York has made an impression on me entirely different from what I had expected. I have found here the most aristocratic sentiments rubbing elbows with the most democratic institutions. I have seen few countries where society is more exclusive, and this exclusiveness is founded on nothing at all. Wealth, political position, and education are not the keys that provide admittance. One is fashionable or one is not, and the why of it is completely unknown to those who are the objects of this preferment and to those who confer it. In my opinion, this is the strangest and often the most unjust social system it is possible to have.

Sig Spaeth
The Advantages of Jay Walking 1926

VISITORS TO NEW YORK will find that both exercise and excitement may be had at a minimum of expense through the simple practice of jay-walking. With only a little experience, they may actually compete on even terms with the native New Yorker.

Only a few fundamental rules need be learned, after which the natural jay-walker can work out as elaborate a technique as may be desired, depending also, of course, upon individual talent and ambition.

One of the first things to be learned is the proper time to start across the street. It is not considered sporting to do this while traffic is standing still. Wait for the policeman's whistle, which is the signal that the cross-current is about to begin. But if you are a stickler for etiquette, take the first step only after the sound of shifting gears has been heard on both sides of the street.

If you get across after that, without having to stop in the middle, you are credited with a perfect score. Failing to complete the distance, however, before a new shifting of the lights, incurs a penalty of one yard at the home curb.

All jay-walkers should learn the feint; with many this is an inborn gift. The suggestion of a sudden dash, abruptly stopped, will often cause a chauffeur to use his four-wheel brakes, with at least three rear-end collisions as a result, during which time the jay-walker can safely advance as much as ten feet, to a position for examining the opposite current of traffic.

Sometimes the simple feint will drive an unsuspecting car directly into a telegraph pole, or, on a wet day, skid it complete around. In either case the feinter is entitled to life membership in the National Association of Jay-Walkers.

Feinting is particularly effective under the Elevated. Here the jay-walker can hide behind a pillar, where he is entirely safe, and by a series of false starts and hasty retreats create quite a lot of excitement.

When an actual crossing is intended, it should be absolutely without warning, for only thus is the pleasure of true sportsmanship assured. Remember always that a car can steer better than a human being, and don't worry about allowing too much room. If you see that a car is actually going to hit you, leap straight into the air, so that, this way, you will at the very least have the driver receive some of the impact.

By following a few such rules, the conscientious jay-walker will soon be trained down to a point where he can safely occupy a six-inch space at any stage of the traffic.

In the making of any such calculations, the handicap of skirts must of course be taken into consideration, but this factor is becoming so negligible that jay-walking may al-

ready be considered a lasting tribute to the equality of the
sexes.

Will Rogers
New Yorkers

NEW YORK IS GETTING LIKE PARIS. Its supposed
devilment is its biggest ad. The rest of the country
drop in here and think that if they don't stay up till four A.M.
that New Yorkers will think they are yokels, when, as a
matter of fact, New Yorkers have been in bed so long, they
don't know what the other half is doing. New York lives off
the out-of-towner trying to make New York think he is quite
a fellow.

THE NORTH

subject—the Itinerary of travelling writers—upon which, as upon so few others, Americans not only feel very strongly, but hold clearcut views that are not befogged by the amiable sentimentalism of the national character. * * *

"No one can know America," said innumerable charming ladies to me, "unless they have seen Atlanta, Georgia," or it may have been Charleston, South Carolina, or Seattle, or the Golden Gate at San Francisco, or Wisconsin, or Martha's Vineyard, or any one of five hundred places each of which seemed to be at least a thousand miles from any of the others. But after a bit I began to get the different attractions classified into sections. Thus in Section One there were five that "of course you will be going to see, Mr. MacDonnell." These were New Orleans, Washington, The Century of Progress Exposition at Chicago, the Grand Canyon of the Colorado River, and the top of the Empire State Building. Whenever Section One was broached, I set my teeth and smiled a sort of smile and swallowed the burning words that I longed to speak, and nodded and said, "Oh, of course I shall be going there," and at last I swore a great and binding oath that I would not visit New Orleans, or Washington, or the Century of Progress Exposition at Chicago, or the Grand Canyon of the Colorado River, or the top of the Empire State Building. Nor did I. The oath was truly kept.

In Section Two came the large towns of the Union, and the advocates of this section tried to make me believe that I would learn about America by visiting Philadelphia, Pittsburgh, Cleveland, Buffalo, Detroit, St. Louis, Kansas City, Rochester, Milwaukee, Cincinnati, and a score of others. But when I enquired in respect of what quality any of these towns was different from any other no one could answer. And when I enquired in respect of what quality any of these beastly new American industrial towns differed from any of our beastly new European industrial towns, again no one could answer. So I, who have seen England's Sheffield, Scotland's Glasgow, France's Lille, Germany's Essen, Italy's Turin, and many another abominable mass of chimneys and slums and hurrying, mean-faced humanity, drew a pencil through the whole of Section Two.

Section Three was much more difficult to deal with, as it was composed of the home-towns either of the people I met at parties, or of the grandfathers or aunts or cousins of the people I met at parties. Thus I was incessantly being called upon to assess in my mind the comparative merits of such places as Burlington, Iowa, Evansville, Indiana, Peoria, Illinois, and Guthrie, Oklahoma. I was given to understand that I had only to set foot in any of them and the town would stop work for the duration of my visit. But it was too difficult to choose from so many, and in the end I had reluctantly to eliminate Section Three.

The Itinerary in Section Four was entirely guided by the letters of introduction with which I was showered in New York. From a study of the august names upon the envelopes of these letters, it appeared that there was no necessity for me to associate on my travels with anyone beneath the rank of a State Governor or the President of a University. Section Four, therefore, was torn up at once, and when I set out at last from New York it was on an Itinerary of my own, combined and dovetailed with three other Itineraries drawn up by the three gentlemen to whom this book is dedicated.

If the Viscount Howe had taken as much trouble over his staff-work when he set out from New York in 1777, he might have obtained more successful results against General Washington.

Well, let's start off on an itinerary of our own, one just as contrary and humorous as old MacDonnell's. It won't stop at every "must" destination, or even at many of the "shoulds." But then places are only excuses for experiences, fun, and points of view, which are the true destinations of this whirlwind tour of the United States.

Let's start by heading north to one of the most famous attractions in the world, Niagara Falls. They say Niagara Falls is mortal, and it may not be as overwhelming a tourist sight as it used to be. But humorists have had quite a time with it for some time now. So put on your raincoat and tiptoe through a few short, divergent observations of America's most spectacular falls.

John Steinbeck
Glad I Saw It 1962

NIAGARA FALLS IS VERY NICE. It's like a large version of the old Bond sign on Times Square. I'm very glad I saw it, because from now on if I am asked whether I have seen Niagara Falls I can say yes, and be telling the truth for once.

Oscar Wilde
Not the Keenest 1883

I WAS DISAPPOINTED WITH NIAGARA—most people must be disappointed with Niagara. Every American bride is taken there, and the sight of the stupendous waterfall must be one of the earliest, if not the keenest disappointments in American married life.

Capt. Basil Hall
Not Disappointed 1829

'DID THE FALLS ANSWER your expectations?' The best answer on this subject I remember to have heard of was made by a gentleman who had just been at Niagara, and on his return was appealed to by a party he met on the way going to the Falls, who naturally asked him, if he thought they would be disappointed. 'Why, no,' said he: 'Not unless you expect to witness the sea coming down from the moon.'

❧*New England has been called many things: puritanical, snooty, stodgy, stuffy, fusty, musty, dusty and, sometimes, quaint. It's . . . well, it's so English: so old, old-fashioned, and wet. It's like one of those blow-up clowns with a big red, rubber nose that just asks to be knocked over, and pops right back up and asks for more.*

British humorist Alex Atkinson starts us off with a drily pointed, English view of the place that kept the name of the parents it kicked out of the house, and then nineteenth-century American humorist Artemus Ward gives a short tour of Boston's famous sights. Next, the great American humorous essayist E. B. White not only visits Walden Pond, but describes it to Thoreau himself. Finally, we take a hapless walk in the wild wilderness known as Massachusetts with British humorist H. F. Ellis.

Alex Atkinson
Upper Right 1959

NEW ENGLAND is up in the top right-hand corner—about as far away from wicked Las Vegas as it can get without actually putting out to sea. It is very old and slightly more historic than Stratford-on-Avon, Warwickshire. I was constantly being shown bits of the *Mayflower,* scenes of bloody massacres by the British, genuine pilgrims' hats marked *Kiss Me Baby,* or the graves of people like Hawthorne, Tom Thumb, Samuel Adams and Louisa May Alcott. In Boston, Mass., which is a place of interest in New England (others being Wiscasset, Skowhegan and the Jethro Coffin House in Nantucket, admission 30¢), I saw the place where Emerson grazed his mother's cow. It seemed an ideal spot. Here too I saw where Paul Revere, a rider, finally crushed the armed might of Britain with a lantern and some Minute Men; and outside the Boston Athenaeum (closed Sat.) an old gentleman with bean-stains on his necktie told me that the planet Jupiter rises five minutes earlier in Boston than it does in Washington. I congratulated him warmly, and made a mental note to see what the position is in Texas.

Artemus Ward
Boston c. 1865

DEAR BETSY: I write you this from Boston, "the Modern Atkins," as it is denomyunated, altho' I skurcely know what those air. I'll giv you a kursoory view of this city. I'll klassify the paragrafs under seprit headins, arter the stile of those Emblems of Trooth and Poority, the Washinton correspongdents!

Copps' Hill.

The winder of my room commands a exileratin view of Copps' Hill, where Cotton Mather, the father of the Reformers and sich, lies berrid. There is men even now who worship Cotton, and there is wimin who wear him next their harts. But I do not weep for him. He's bin ded too lengthy. I ain't going to be absurd, like old Mr. Skillins, in our naber-hood, who is ninety-six years of age, and gets drunk every 'lection day, and weeps Bitturly because he haint got no Parents. He's a nice Orphan, *he* is.

The Common.

It is here, as ushil; and the low cuss who called it a Wacant Lot, and wanted to know why they didn't ornament it with sum Bildins', is a onhappy Outcast in Naponsit.

Harvard College.

This celebrated institootion of learnin' is pleasantly situated in the Bar-room of Parker's, in School street, and has poopils from all over the country.

Where the fust blud was spilt.

I went over to Lexington yes'd'y. My Boosum hove with sollum emotions. "& this," I said to a man who was drivin' a yoke of oxen, "this is where our revolutionary forefathers asserted their independence and spilt their Blud. Classic ground!"

"Wall," the man said, "it's good for white beans and potatoes, but as regards raisin' wheat, t'ain't worth a damn."

Your Own Troo husban',

Artemus Ward.

125

E. B. White
Walden 1942

MISS NIMS, take a letter to Henry David Thoreau. Dear Henry: I thought of you the other afternoon as I was approaching Concord doing fifty on Route 62. That is a high speed at which to hold a philosopher in one's mind, but in this century we are a nimble bunch.

On one of the lawns in the outskirts of the village a woman was cutting the grass with a motorized lawn mower. What made me think of you was that the machine had rather got away from her, although she was game enough, and in the brief glimpse I had of the scene it appeared to me that the lawn was mowing the lady. She kept a tight grip on the handles, which throbbed violently with every explosion of the one-cylinder motor, and as she sheered around bushes and lurched along at a reluctant trot behind her impetuous servant, she looked like a puppy who had grabbed something that was too much for him. Concord hasn't changed much, Henry; the farm implements and the animals still have the upper hand.

I may as well admit that I was journeying to Concord with the deliberate intention of visiting your woods; for although I have never knelt at the grave of a philosopher nor placed wreaths on moldy poets, and have often gone a mile out of my way to avoid some place of historical interest, I have always wanted to see Walden Pond. The account which you left of your sojourn there is, you will be amused to learn, a document of increasing pertinence; each year it seems to gain a little headway, as the world loses ground. We may all be transcendental yet, whether we like it or not. As our common complexities increase, any tale of individual simplicity (and yours is the best written and the cockiest) acquires a new fascination; as our goods accumulate, but

126

not our well-being, your report of an existence without material adornment takes on a certain awkward credibility.

My purpose in going to Walden Pond, like yours, was not to live cheaply or to live dearly there, but to transact some private business with the fewest obstacles. Approaching Concord, doing forty, doing forty-five, doing fifty, the steering wheel held snug in my palms, the highway held grimly in my vision, the crown of the road now serving me (on the righthand curves), now defeating me (on the lefthand curves), I began to rouse myself from the stupefaction which a day's motor journey induces. It was a delicious evening, Henry, when the whole body is one sense, and imbibes delight through every pore, if I may coin a phrase. Fields were richly brown where the harrow, drawn by the stripped Ford, had lately sunk its teeth; pastures were green; and overhead the sky had that same everlasting great look which you will find on Page 144 of the Oxford pocket edition. I could feel that road entering me, through tire, wheel, spring, and cushion; shall I not have intelligence with earth too? Am I not partly leaves and vegetable mold myself?—a man of infinite horsepower, yet partly leaves.

Stay with me on 62 and it will take you into Concord. As I say, it was a delicious evening. The snake had come forth to die in a bloody S on the highway, the wheel upon its head, its bowels flat now and exposed. The turtle had come up too to cross the road and die in the attempt, its hard shell smashed under the rubber blow, its intestinal yearning (for the other side of the road) forever squashed. There was a sign by the wayside which announced that the road had a "cotton surface." You wouldn't know what that is, but neither, for that matter, did I. There is a cryptic ingredient in many of our modern improvements—we are awed and pleased without knowing quite what we are enjoying. It is something to be traveling on a road with a cotton surface.

The civilization round Concord to-day is an odd distillation of city, village, farm, and manor. The houses, yards, fields look not quite suburban, not quite rural. Under the bronze beech and the blue spruce of the departed baron grazes the milch goat of the heirs. Under the porte-cochère stands the reconditioned station wagon; under the grape arbor sit the puppies for sale. (But why do men degenerate ever? What makes families run out?)

It was June and everywhere June was publishing her immemorial stanza; in the lilacs, in the syringa, in the freshly edged paths and the sweetness of moist beloved gardens, and the little wire wickets that preserve the tulips' front. Farmers were already moving the fruits of their toil into their yards, arranging the rhubarb, the asparagus, the strictly fresh eggs on the painted stands under the little shed roofs with the patent shingles. And though it was almost a hundred years since you had taken your ax and started cutting out your home on Walden Pond, I was interested to observe that the philosophical spirit was still alive in Massachusetts: in the center of a vacant lot some boys were assembling the framework of a rude shelter, their whole mind and skill concentrated in the rather inauspicious helter-skelter of studs and rafters. They too were escaping from town, to live naturally, in a rich blend of savagery and philosophy. * * *

Next morning early I started afoot for Walden, out Main Street and down Thoreau, past the depot and the Minute-man Chevrolet Company. The morning was fresh, and in a bean field along the way I flushed an agriculturalist, quietly studying his beans. Thoreau Street soon joined Number 126, an artery of the State. We number our highways nowadays, our speed being so great we can remember little of their quality or character and are lucky to remember their number. (Men have an indistinct notion that if they keep up this activity long enough all will at length ride somewhere, in next to no time.) Your pond is on 126.

I knew I must be nearing your woodland retreat when the Golden Pheasant lunchroom came into view—Sealtest ice cream, toasted sandwiches, hot frankfurters, waffles, tonics, and lunches. Were I the proprietor, I should add rice,

Indian meal, and molasses—just for old time's sake. The Pheasant, incidentally, is for sale: a chance for some nature lover who wishes to set himself up beside a pond in the Concord atmosphere and live deliberately, fronting only the essential facts of life on Number 126. Beyond the Pheasant was a place called Walden Breezes, an oasis whose porch pillars were made of old green shutters sawed into lengths. On the porch was a distorting mirror, to give the traveler a comical image of himself, who had miraculously learned to gaze in an ordinary glass without smiling. Behind the Breezes, in a sun-parched clearing, dwelt your philosophical descendants in their trailers, each trailer the size of your hut, but all grouped together for the sake of congeniality. Trailer people leave the city, as you did, to discover solitude and in any weather, at any hour of the day or night, to improve the nick of time; but they soon collect in villages and get bogged deeper in the mud than ever. . .

Leaving the highway I turned off into the woods toward the pond, which was apparent through the foliage. The floor of the forest was strewn with dried old oak leaves and *Transcripts*. From beneath the flattened popcorn wrapper *(granum explosum)* peeped the frail violet. I followed a footpath and descended to the water's edge. The pond lay clear and blue in the morning light, as you have seen it so many times. In the shallows a man's waterlogged shirt undulated gently. A few flies came out to greet me and convoy me to your cove, past the No Bathing signs on which the fellows and the girls had scrawled their names. I felt strangely excited suddenly to be snooping around your premises, tiptoeing along watchfully, as though not to tread by mistake upon the intervening century. Before I got to the cove I heard something which seemed to me quite wonderful: I heard your frog, a full, clear *troonk,* guiding me, still hoarse and solemn, bridging the years as the robins had bridged them in the sweetness of the village evening. But he soon quit, and I came on a couple of your boys throwing stones at him.

Your front yard is marked by a bronze tablet set in a stone. Four small granite posts, a few feet away, show where the house was. On top of the tablet was a pair of faded blue bathing trunks with a white stripe. Back of it is a pile of stones, a sort of cairn, left by your visitors as a tribute I suppose. It is a rather ugly little heap of stones, Henry. In fact the hillside itself seems faded, browbeaten; a few tall skinny pines, bare of lower limbs, a smattering of your maples in suitable green, some birches and oaks, and a number of trees felled by the last big wind. It was from the bole of one of these fallen pines, torn up by the roots, that I extracted the stone which I added to the cairn—a sentimental act in which I was interrupted by a small terrier from a nearby picnic group, who confronted me and wanted to know about the stone.

I sat down for a while on one of the posts of your house to listen to the bluebottles and the dragonflies. The invaded glade sprawled shabby and mean at my feet, but the flies were tuned to the old vibration. There were the remains of a fire in your ruins, but I doubt that it was yours; also two beer bottles trodden into the soil and become part of earth. A young oak had taken root in your house, and two or three ferns, unrolling like the ticklers at a banquet. The only other furnishings were a DuBarry pattern sheet, a page torn from a picture magazine, and some crusts in wax paper.

Before I quit I walked clear round the pond and found the place where you used to sit on the northeast side to get the sun in the fall, and the beach where you got sand for scrubbing your floor. On the eastern side of the pond, where the highway borders it, the State has built dressing rooms for swimmers, a float with diving towers, drinking fountains of porcelain, and rowboats for hire. The pond is in fact a State Preserve, and carries a twenty-dollar fine for picking wild flowers, a decree signed in all solemnity by your fellow-citizens Walter C. Wardwell, Erson B. Barlow, and Nathaniel I. Bowditch. There was a smell of creosote where they had been building a wide wooden stairway to the road and the parking area. Swimmers and boaters were arriving; bodies plunged vigorously into the water and emerged wet and beautiful in the bright air. As I left, a boatload of town boys were splashing about in mid-pond, kidding and fooling, the young fellows singing at the tops of their lungs in a wild chorus:

> Amer-ica, Amer-i-ca, God shed his grace on thee,
> And crown thy good with brotherhood
> From sea to shi-ning sea!

I walked back to town along the railroad, following your custom. The rails were expanding noisily in the hot sun, and on the slope of the roadbed the wild grape and the black-berry sent up their creepers to the track.

H. F. Ellis
A Walk in Massachusetts   1960

FOR THE STATE OF NEAR PANIC I got into last spring, in a wood about five miles from Groton, Massachusetts, I am indebted, in the main, to John Hersey, Clifford H. Pope, and a lady in a small sports car. The lady took me to the wood. "If you are interested in birds," she told me, "it's the ideal place. A kind of nature preserve. Nobody ever goes there, so you'll be quite undisturbed, and herons nest on the island." She had found me beside the road, in a pleasant, swampy area just across the Ayer-Hollis branch freight railroad line, had offered me a ride, and had quickly discovered that I was British and a bird watcher.

"It is extremely kind of you to bother," I said. It is always extremely kind of Americans to bother, and no counter has yet been devised by visiting Englishmen to stop them from doing it.

We drove for a couple of miles along tarmac roads, branched off on a dirt road between farmsteads, and jogged and jolted down a rutted sand track into a forest of conifers. A pair of what I thought might be red-shouldered hawks wheeled in the flawless June sky. The track ended at a stretch of sluggish backwater, and there I got out. I had only to follow the river to the left, the lady told me, and I would find that it curled round on itself and would, in time, lead me back to the main road. "Look out for poison ivy!" she called as she turned the car. "There's a lot of it in these woods."

"Right," I said. "Thanks. Oh, by the way— I say— How does one—"

"It kind of grows in threes," she cried, waved, and was gone.

It was intensely hot. No breath of air penetrated the close-set trees. Nothing moved, and no birds sang. An island across the water appeared to be heronless. There was, however, a discernible path running by the water's edge, and I was glad to follow it. Poison ivy does not grow in Britain, nor did I recollect much about it save that it is not recognizable as ivy and that its lightest touch leads to intense irritation, bloating of the body, and possible collapse. But a man who walks with circumspection along a path, keeping in the middle of it and on no account sitting down to rest, has little to fear. I pressed forward, holding the arms close to the body and noting, without excitement, some curious round bumps on a derelict tree trunk half submerged in the water. My mind was occupied at this time with the need for tobacco and with the obvious folly of lighting a cigarette in this crackling tinderbox of a forest.

The bumps slid off and poised themselves an inch or so below the surface, extruding stringy necks and bluntish yellow heads. I watched them with mounting interest. America is full of differences for an Englishman. New York is instantly distinguishable from London. Lobster tastes better. The Budd Highliner, on its run from Boston to Ayer, makes a wailing noise at crossings that would never be tolerated in England. But these differences are neither unexpected nor radical. Turtles are something else altogether. Turtles are downright un-English. Free, wild, and treading water gently by an old tree trunk, they affect the mind far more powerfully than a Pullman-car attendant or even a copy of the *Herald Tribune*. For the first time, looking at them, I became aware that I was on a vast continent—exotic, tropical, rich in the possibility of surprises undreamed of in Shropshire or Kent.

I was not in any way frightened. The British, for all their loss of prestige, are not yet afraid of small turtles. The note that I immediately made, on the flyleaf of my pocket "Field Guide to the Birds (Eastern)," is in front of me now, and the writing is, for a man menaced by poison ivy and with sweat trickling off his nose, admirably firm. "Yellow on head," it reads. "Red on neck and at sides of shell. Fond of sunning. Submerges when startled." It is the first field note I ever made on turtles, and for identification purposes is insufficiently detailed. But at the time I thought it would do. Back at home, I had recently acquired a book by Clifford H. Pope, with descriptions and photographs of innumerable species of turtles; somewhere there, I thought, these yellow-headed turtles would be.

My mind associates very readily when I am alone in great heat in foreign woods. It would have been difficult, whatever the circumstances, to recall Clifford H. Pope's turtles without reflecting that the same fine volume, "The Reptile World," contains about a hundred photographs of snakes. Pretty nearly all of them flashed on my mental retina simultaneously. Not all, of course, infest America. Cobras I could shrug off, and also, I rather hoped, the dreaded Russell's viper. But there were plenty left. With particular vividness, there recurred to me a picture of a long, thin snake looped and coiled about a branch, and some excellent high-speed photographs of a rattlesnake striking a balloon. Just such a target would be provided, coincidentally, by a man under the influence of poison ivy. . . .

Preoccupied with these thoughts, I failed to notice that the conifers had receded and the path had petered out. All about me were deciduous trees whose branches trailed curious, often trifoliate, parasitical growths. Between their trunks grew low bushes and taller shrubs, mostly in kind of threes, while underfoot the ground lay deep in the debris, the leaf mold and withered branches, of centuries of decay, so that it was hard to tell where best to tread. Some sort of willows, their gnarled roots suggestive of alligators, drooped over the stagnant waters.

I am glad to think that I retained, at this stage, a sense of proportion. It could be that of all the countless varieties of venomous snakes indigenous to America so sinuously described by Mr. Pope, no more than three or four were ever found in Massachusetts. "A Field Guide to the Snakes (Eastern)" might be an altogether slimmer volume than my bird book. As for the poison ivy, a touch of cutaneous eruption would be a small price to pay for a glimpse of the island where herons once nested. Still, I thought it best to turn the cuffs of my trousers down over my ankles, in case the ivy was a ground creeper. I kept my hands in my pockets against the risk of waist-high bushes. For the exposed face and neck, nothing could be done except to keep a constant watch for trailing growths when passing under trees; I should be looking up in any case, because no naturalist wants to miss his first sight of a long, thin snake looped and coiled about a branch. The difficulty here was that the urge to look down was no less strong. "Watch where you step" was a phrase that came back to me from Clifford H. Pope's useful section on snake-bite prevention and treatment.

I suppose that any resident of Groton who had seen me mincing along thus protected, looking down and up before every step and shrinking away with loathing from every vegetable contact, would have laughed uproariously. The lady with the sports car would have been in stitches. Local knowledge makes a world of difference. Here in England, where a mild rash from the stinging nettle is the gravest probable consequence of a country walk, I stride along as briskly as any Grotonian. I should have done the same, I daresay, in Massachusetts had I read Mr. Pope's book more carefully (or not at all), or had the lady in the sports car not been kind enough to bother.

Oddly, it was neither of these two that finally broke my nerve. It happened that in swerving away from a particularly vicious three-pronged attack from overhead I put my foot on some round, slippery object (perhaps a dead branch) and, so rapidly was my mind associating by this time, I actually recalled a whole passage from John Hersey's novel "The Marmot Drive" while still in the act of falling backward into a prehensile bush of a type not found on my side of the Atlantic. By pure chance, not having the gift of divination, I had borrowed this book from the ship's library on my way over to the United States. It is recommended reading for anyone not contemplating a walk in Massachusetts. For me, it would have been better had the scene of the great round-up of groundhogs been set in some other state; better still if the heroine had not fallen into a thicket during the drive.

She was not, of course, actually eaten alive by ground-hogs. She was not even afraid of being eaten alive, because she knew that some of her friends in the long line of beaters ahead would soon notice her absence and come thrashing back. She was a calm, sensible sort of girl, and soon realized that the more she struggled the more deeply she would enmesh herself in the spiny thicket. So she just lay still and waited. I was unable to emulate her confident self-possession. One of the delights of a nature preserve, as the sports-car lady had pointed out, is that nobody ever goes there.

It would be wrong to give the impression that I remained on my back for any length of time, or that I seriously expected to be attacked by groundhogs. I suppose I was on my feet again within ten seconds. What really distressed me was the rate at which my fears were multiplying in these unfamiliar surroundings. At any moment, I would trip over an anthill and start reciting from "The Cocktail Party." I had come out for an enjoyable country ramble, and already it seemed doubtful, unless I took a firm grip of myself, whether I should get any enjoyment out of it at all.

It is not easy to take a grip of yourself when there is nothing to grip *against*. If a pack of wolves had come padding through the trees, I daresay I should have attacked them with almost foolhardy courage. A single puma might have made a man of me. But the silence, the sinister absence of visible life of any kind continued unbroken. I had to fight this thing unaided, with psychological weapons. "What kind of a fool are you?" I asked myself. "Do you really imagine you are in any danger, here within five miles of America's most exclusive school?" The answer I gave to that was yes. Very well, then, I argued, go on from there; let your imagination run riot and see where it gets you. Suppose that the worst has happened, and try to visualize the consequences. My family would have to be informed. There would be a cable, sooner or later. I called up a picture of my London home, heard the crunch of the telegraph boy's wheels on the driveway, saw my wife at the door taking the buff envelope from his gauntleted hands. I saw her slit the envelope and take out the flimsy form. "REGRET TO INFORM YOU YOUR HUSBAND EATEN BY GROUNDHOGS NEAR GROTON. DETAILS FOLLOW. DO YOU WISH REMAINS EXPRESSED TO ENGLAND?"

This *reductio-ad-absurdum* method has much to commend it. Make a mockery of one's fears and they dissolve in laughter. I have known it to work with more normal everyday worries. But I overdid it. I got sidetracked on the word "REMAINS." I could not help wondering, from what I remembered of Hersey on the voraciousness of groundhogs, whether much—supposing I blundered into a really thick thicket—would be left. Perhaps only the flexible portions of my shoes? It even crossed my mind that I possibly ought to write my name on the soles, for identification purposes.

This was my lowest ebb. There is a pit of abasement that, once reached, practically abolishes fear. A man who has descended to the point of writing on his shoes no longer cares. Thus, in a strangely indirect way, my psychological one form or another, every hour of the day. "I tell you, I was just an ordinary fellow, with an ordinary fellow's interest in the Civil War, until I spent two days at Gettysburg," an ordinary fellow who gave the impression of having been through a protracted siege said not long ago. "Now I think I could lecture at the War College. It all began when I took a room in a motel on the edge of the battlefield. This particular motel lay almost directly in the line of Pickett's Charge—athwart it, you might say. Pickett's Charge, of course, was the unsuccessful offensive mounted by the Confederate troops on the afternoon of July 3rd, when Pickett and his men marched out from the Confederate left flank on Seminary Ridge and crossed an open field to meet the Union troops head on on Cemetery Ridge. I would place the start of the charge at approximately 3 P.M., Eastern Standard Time. I won't go so far as to say that Pickett's men would have come right *through* my bedroom, but they might well have bruised themselves on the television set against my southern wall. Actually, I feel certain that Pettigrew's men— he was stationed to the left of Pickett—and the men of Archer, Davis, Scales, and Lane would have come right across my bed, knocking over the telephone and the bed lamp. They ran into Meade's men—Hays, Webb, Gibbon, and the rest—and at the Angle it was bloody beyond description, and the Confederates were turned back at the Copse of Trees, at what is known as the High Water Mark of the Confederacy. The Rebels were said to be incapable of ever again mounting an offensive. Pickett's Charge was all over by ten minutes to four, but I kept going in Gettysburg pretty much around the clock, taking bus rides with built-in sound effects describing every last inch of the battle, watching an electric map with hundreds of little lights blinking and winking to show the position of the troops, looking at a cyclorama of the battle, walking over the battlefield, taking a guided tour in my own car, with a hired guide, and buying toy cannons, old bullets, flags, literature of all sorts, and tons of picture postcards. Now, if I had been Pickett. . ."

The sense of history that pervades the city often produces an anesthetic effect that can take days to shake off. This happens most often to people who hire an official guide to accompany them as they drive around the thirty-odd square miles that constitute the battlefield. Groups of these guides—elderly men, for the most part—sit and sun themselves in front of small stone houses that are scattered about the edge of the field. Many of the guides would make interesting picture postcards. They leave the impression that they are veterans of the battle. They are staggering repositories of information, much of it in the general area of blood and gore. They feel that, seated beside a person who has hired their services for an hour or an hour and a half while he drives along the quiet tree-lined and gun-lined roads, they have a duty to dwell upon the horrors of war. Actually, bodies no longer lie out on the gently rolling, alternately brown and green fields, but the guides are corpse-conscious just the same, and they cannot pass a gully, an open stretch, or a battery of guns without making vivid references to the toll of human life that was taken at Gettysburg. They savor casualty figures, and roll them over and over on their tongues, with special attention to the number of hours or days that "the dead lay out there in the hot sun." Nor is their arithmetical ardor confined to casualty figures. The cost of various monuments titillates them to a frenzy of statistics, and they cite to the penny the amount expended on every monument they pass. "When I got through with one of those guides," a visitor to Gettysburg remarked recently, "I had the feeling that I had been driving around with a man from Price Waterhouse who had come to the field, eagle-eyed, to examine the books." Most of the guides are brigadiers *manqué*, or at least colonels *manqué*, possessed of a mysterious, superior untapped skill in commanding vast armies of men over broad areas under optimum conditions of strategy and tactics. They find it difficult to concede that the generals who fought the battle knew what they were doing, and they make it clear that if

139

♠The South

♠*To foreigners, northerners, and westerners, the South is a magical land of honor and hospitality, drawls and plantations, tall women and long memories. Is it all in our minds? Do southerners just have good PR and not a mint julep between them? Well, there's no myth like a good myth, and the South's got one of the best around.*

I looked far to the north to find someone who could put his finger on what makes the South the South. In fact, so far to the north that I ended up with a Canadian, Stephen Leacock, the only economist with a truly great sense of humor.

Once we've been introduced to the South, Julian Street will examine its deepest, darkest mystery: is 'you-all' singular or plural? And then we'll start heading south, with stops in Washington with American novelist Allen Drury and classic American humorist Will Rogers; and Virginia with British novelist William Golding.

Stephen Leacock
Complete Guide and History
of the South 1926

Based on the Best Models of Travelers' Impressions——

IN SETTING DOWN HERE my impression of southern life, southern character, southern industry, and what I am led to call the soul of the southern people, I am compelled to admit that these impressions are necessarily incomplete. The time at my disposal—twenty-four hours less fifteen minutes while I was shaving—was, as I myself felt, inadequate for the purpose.

I could have spent double, nay treble, nay quadruple the time in the South with profit, and could have secured twice, nay three times, nay four times as many impressions. At the same time I may say in apology that my impressions, such as they are, are based on the very best models of travelers' impressions which are published in such floods by visitors to this continent.

To one who has the eye to see it, the journey south from New York to Washington, which may be called the capital of the United States, is filled with interest. The broad farm lands of New Jersey, the view of the city of Philadelphia, and the crossing of the spacious waters of the Susquehanna, offer a picture well worth carrying away. Unfortunately I did not see it. It was night when I went through. But I read about it in the railroad folder next morning.

After passing Washington the traveler finds himself in the country of the Civil War, where the landscape recalls at every turn the great struggle of sixty years ago. Here is the Acquia Creek and here is Fredericksburg, the scene of one of the most disastrous defeats of the northern armies. I missed it, I am sorry to say. I was eating lunch and didn't see it. But the porter told me that we had passed Fredericksburg.

It is however with a certain thrill that one finds oneself passing Richmond, the home of the Lost Cause, where there still lingers all the romance of the glory that once was. Unluckily our train didn't go by Richmond but straight south via Lynchburg Junction. But if it had I might have seen it.

As one continues the journey southward, one realizes that one is in the South. The conviction was gradually borne in on me as I kept going south that I was getting South. It is an impression, I believe, which all travelers have noted in proportion as they proceed South.

I could not help saying to myself, "I am now in the South." It is a feeling I have never had in the North. As I looked from the train window I could not resist remarking, "So this is the South." I have every reason to believe that it was.

One becomes conscious of a difference of life, of atmosphere, of the character of the people. The typical southerner is courteous, chivalrous, with an old-world air about him. I noted that on asking one of my fellow travelers for a match he responded, "I am deeply sorry, I fear I have none. I had a match in my other pants yesterday, but I left them at home. Perhaps I could go back and get them."

Another gentleman in the smoking room of whom I ventured to ask the time replied, "I am deeply sorry, I have no watch. But if you will wait till we get to the next station, I will get out and buy a clock and let you know." I thanked him, but thought it the part of good taste to refuse his offer.

Every day one hears everywhere reminiscences and talk of the Civil War. Nearly everybody with whom I fell into conversation—and I kept falling into it—had something to say or to recall about the days of Lee and Jackson and of what I may call the Southern Confederacy.

One old gentleman told me that he remembered the war as if it were yesterday, having participated in a number of the great episodes of the struggle. He told me that after General Lee had been killed at Gettysburg, Andrew Jackson was almost in despair; and yet had the Southerners only known it, there was at the time only a thin screen of two hundred thousand union troops between them and Washington.

In the light of these conversations and reminiscences it was interesting presently to find oneself in Georgia and to realize that one was traversing the ground of Sherman's famous march to the sea. Unluckily for me, it was night when we went through, but I knew where we were because during a temporary stoppage of the train, I put my head out of the curtains and said to the porter, "Where are we?" and he answered, "Georgia." As I looked out into the profound darkness that enveloped us, I realized as never before the difficulty of Sherman's task.

At this point, perhaps it may be well to say something of the women of the South, a topic without which no impression would be worth publishing. The southern women, one finds, are distinguished everywhere by their dignity and reserve. (Two women came into the Pullman car where I was, and when I offered one of them an apple she wouldn't take it.) But they possess at the same time a charm and graciousness that is all their own. (When I said to the other woman that it was a good deal warmer than it had been she smiled and said that it certainly was.)

The Southern woman is essentially womanly and yet entirely able to look after herself. (These two went right into the dining car by themselves without waiting for me or seeming to want me.) Of the beauty of the Southern type there can be no doubt. (I saw a girl with bobbed-hair on the platform at Danville, but when I waved to her even her hair would not wave.)

On the morning following we found ourselves approaching Birmingham, Alabama. On looking at it out of the car window, I saw at once that Birmingham contains a population of 200,000 inhabitants, having grown greatly in the last decade; that the town boasts not less than sixteen churches and several large hotels of the modern type.

I saw also that it is rapidly becoming a seat of manufacture, possessing in 1921 not less than 14,000 spindles, while its blast furnaces bid fair to rival those of Pittsburgh, Pennsylvania and Hangkow, China; I noticed that the leading denomination is Methodist, both white and colored, but the Roman Catholic, the Episcopalian and other churches are also represented. The town, as I saw at a glance, enjoys exceptional educational opportunities, the enrollment of pupils in the high schools numbering half a million.

The impression which I carried away from Birmingham enabled me to form some idea (that is all I ever get) of the new economic growth of the South. Everywhere one sees evidence of the fertility of the soil and the relative ease of sustenance. (I saw a man buy a whole bunch of bananas and eat them right in the car.) The growth of wealth is remarkable. (I noticed a man hand out a fifty dollar bill in the dining car and get change as if it were nothing.)

I had originally intended to devote my time after leaving Birmingham to the investigation and analysis of the *soul* of the South, for which I had reserved four hours. Unfortunately I was not able to do so. I got called in to join a poker game in the drawing room and it lasted all the way to New Orleans.

But even in the imperfect form in which I have been able to put together these memoirs of travel I feel on looking over them that they are all right, or at least as good as the sort of stuff that is handed out every month in the magazines.

Julian Street
Am I You-All? 1917

ONCE SUCH MATTERS AS THESE are fully understood in the North, there will be left but one grave issue between North and South, that issue being over the question of whether or not Southerners, under any circumstances, use the phrase "you-all" in the singular.

"Whatever you write of the South," said our hostess at a dinner party in Virginia, "don't make the mistake of representing any one from this paht of the country, white or black, educated oh ignorant, as saying 'you-all' meaning one person only."

When I remarked mildly that it seemed to me I had often seen the phrase so used in books, and heard it in plays, eight or ten southern ladies and gentlemen at the table pounced upon me, all at once. "Yes!" they agreed, with a kind of polite violence, "books and plays by Yankees!"

"If," one of the gentlemen explained, "you write to a

friend who has a family, and say, according to the northern practice, 'I hope to see you when you come to my town,' you write something which is really ambiguous, since the word 'you' may refer only to your friend, or may refer also to his family. Our southern 'you-all' makes it explicit."

I told him that in the North we also used the word "all" in connection with "you," though we accented the two evenly, and did not compound them, but he seemed to believe that "you" followed by "all" belonged exclusively to the South.

The argument continued almost constantly throughout the meal. Not until coffee was served did the subject seem to be exhausted. But it was not, for after pouring a demi-tasse our hostess lifted a lump of sugar in the tongs, and looking me directly in the eye inquired: "Do you-all take sugah?"

Undoubtedly it would have been wiser, and politer, to let this pass, but the discussion had filled me with curiosity, not only because of my interest in the localism, but also because of the amazing intensity with which it had been discussed.

"But," I exclaimed, "you just said 'you-all,' apparently addressing me. Didn't you use it in the singular?"

No sooner had I spoken than I was sorry. Every one looked disconcerted. There was silence for a moment. I was very much ashamed.

"Oh, no," she said at last. "When I said 'you-all' I meant you and Mr. Morgan." (She pronounced it "Moh-gan," with a lovely drawl.) As she made this statement, she blushed, poor lady!

Being to blame for her discomfiture, I could not bear to see her blush, and looked away, but only to catch the eye of my companion, and to read in its evil gleam the thought: "Of course they use it in the singular. But aren't you ashamed of having tripped up such a pretty creature on a point of dialect?"

Though my interest in the southern idiom had caused me to forget about the sugar, my hostess had not forgotten.

"Well," she said, still balancing the lump above the cup, and continuing gamely to put the question in the same form, and to me: "Do you-all take sugah, oh not?"

I had no idea how my companion took his coffee, but it seemed to me that tardy politeness now demanded that I tacitly—or at least demi-tacitly—accede to the alleged plural intent of the question. Therefore, I replied: "Mr. Morgan takes two lumps. I don't take any, thanks."

Late that night as we were returning to our hotel, my companion said to me somewhat tartly: "In case such a thing comes up again, I wish you would remember that sugar in my coffee makes me ill."

"Well, why didn't you say so?"

"Because," he returned, "I thought that you-all ought to do the answering. It seemed best for me-all to keep quiet and try to look plural under the singular conditions."

Allen Drury
The Tourist Capital 1959

THE VOICE OF THE TOURIST is heard in the land. At this very moment on this brightly sparkling morning he is arising in his thousands in his myriad hotels, motels, and other temporary warrens and gathering himself together for another day of mass assault upon the noble monuments and busy offices of his government. There will be some of his kind who will make the excursion with friends or relatives; some who will take guided tours in sight-seeing buses; and still others who will start out on their own with cameras, dogged determination, and a rather hazy concept of what they will find. "Where does the President work?" some of them will ask when they go through the Capitol. "We've seen the Senate and the House, now can you tell us where we can see Congress?"

The first wave is here, tramping with weary tenacity through the Smithsonian and the Zoo, paying their hasty camera-clicking tributes to Abe Lincoln in his temple ("Stand over there by his right foot, Kit,"), allowing half an hour for a quick run through the National Gallery of Art, hurrying one another along in a pushing, shoving, exclaiming line through Mount Vernon, the White House, and Lee House in Arlington, peeking in quickly at the massive red-draped chamber of the Supreme Court, viewing with suitable awe the blood-stained relics of the FBI, ascending the Washington Monument for a glimpse, all too brief, of the city, the river, the surrounding countryside, all the monuments and buildings, the great scheme of L'Enfant laid out before them with its broad avenues, its carpeting of tree tops everywhere, its veneer of world capital still not effacing a certain gracious, comfortable, small-town aspect that not all the problems nor all the tourists in Christendom can quite obscure.

The city has prepared itself for the onslaught by a sort of instinctive battening down of the hatches. "Just wait until the tourists come," people have been saying warningly to one another for weeks; or, "Well, I guess if we can't make it now we'd better wait until fall, because the tourists will be here in a little while and you know what a mess that is." Yet it is not done unkindly, nor is it entirely devoid of appreciation for the excitement of those who visit for the first time. There are enough who can remember their own first days here, when all the streets were golden and everyone who passed was ten feet tall and bound upon secret missions of high import. Although the streets have long since returned to asphalt and the unmoved eyes of experience now see that most of those who pass are not ten feet tall but just tired little government workers worrying about the mortgage, something of the aura lingers still; and so the visitors are patiently suffered and forgiven much.

Will Rogers
While the Cats're Away 1927

WASHINGTON, D. C., AUG. 26. — Tourists, you are missing something if you don't visit Washington while the politicians are not here. You have no idea the difference it makes. The bootleggers have followed their constituents back home. The embassy bars are closed; even Washington's national pest, the lobbyists, have gone home to take up another collection. Why, if they could get this Capitol moved away from here this would be one of the best towns in America. I think there are people in this city smart enough to vote.

William Golding
One Eye Open—At Most 1965

I DON'T KNOW HOW FAR the Alleghanies stretch. They are the small patch of brown, half-way up the map of America on the right-hand side. They consist of parallel ranges, and cover, I suppose, more area than the British Isles. They are not very distinguished as mountains go. They are relatively low, and tree-clad. They have no violence, but abundant charm. How should they not? They pass through Virginia, where charm is laid on so thick you could saw it off in chunks and export it.

Here, in Virginia, is none of the restless energy, the determined modernity, the revolutionary fervour, which in retrospect I see to have characterized my own country. I crossed the Atlantic from the passionate antagonisms of Salisbury traffic on a market day, to the controlled silence of New York in a rush hour. New York traffic flows in a tide too full for sound or foam, and is peaceful by comparison. I thought then that the allegedly horrifying pace of American life was a European invention; and when I got to

Virginia I was certain of it. Shout at Virginia, shake it, slap its face, jump on it — Virginia will open one eye, smile vaguely, and go to sleep again.

Our base of operations is Hollins, a rich girls' college, lapped about by fields, and set down in a fold of the Alleghanies. It is ineffably peaceful. Wherever you look, there are hills looped along the skyline. Every circumstance pleases, woos, soothes, and makes comprehension difficult. We arrived during the Indian summer, when every blade of grass, every leaf, was loaded down with cicadas, each of which seemed to be operating a small dentist's drill. Eagles and buzzards floated a thousand feet up in the hot air. Blue jays played in the fields and a delicately built mocking-bird balanced on the white fence by our window like a lady with a parasol on a tightrope. On the day of our arrival, a mountain bear—probably walking in his sleep—wandered into the nearby town, saw himself in the glass door of the library, panicked, woke up the neighbourhood, was anaesthetized and taken home again. * * *

Here, then, we work gently, with cushions under us, and plate glass between us and the rest of the world. It is pleasant to contemplate the clock on the administration building, by which we regulate our affairs. For the clock is a Virginian Clock. The minute hand toils up, lifting the heavy weight of the hour until it totters upright. Then, as if that effort had exhausted the mechanism, the hand falls down to half past three and stays there, collapsed. Long may it continue so to make a mock of the arbitrary, enslaving time-stream! It is as useless and decorative as the carillon which tinkles out Mozart minuets, or hymns, or snatches of old song, from the chapel spire.

To most tourists, Tennessee no longer conjures up pictures of hillbillies or of enormous dam projects and the lakes they created. In fact, Tennessee doesn't conjure up pictures at all, but sounds. The sounds of music, country music especially. And Elvis Presley. No tour of America would be complete without stopping at an Elvis Presley attraction. People might trek up to the Dakota (in that unDakotaish city of New York) to see where John Lennon was shot, but people can travel all over America to see where Elvis was born, sang, acted, and lived. And, after all, John Lennon was British.

Mark Winegardner
See Elvis! 1987

NEAR THE KENTUCKY-TENNESSEE LINE, we first noticed the billboards. And a good 25 miles before we got to Gatlinburg, Tennessee, the billboards took over. VISIT GATLINBURG'S WAX MUSEUM, one red-white-and-blue sign said, and a little square within it invited America's tourists to "See ELVIS!!" Then came one for Silver Dollar City, featuring a grizzled prospector panning for gold in a rock-choked stream and staking a claim to "The Best Variety of Family Attractions." And so it went, with boards for Porpoise Island, the House of Illusions, Stars Over Gatlinburg Wax Museum, Ripley's Believe It or Not Museum, Guinness Book of World Records Museum and the Smoky Mountain Auto Museum, which employed 10-foot-tall letters to boast about its possession of Sheriff Buford T. Pusser's Death Car.

"If Lady Bird Johnson goes to hell," Bob said, "I'll bet they make her spend every day driving down a replica of this road."

Giant water slides and elaborate miniature golf courses lined the highway as we entered Pigeon Forge, Gatlinburg's northern suburb. On the right, beside a package liquor store and a Spur gas station, was a green, two-story motor lodge. When I saw the sign for the place, I had no choice but to pull El Basurero into the parking lot.

ELVIS MUSEUM, read the top part of the huge sign, a royal blue crown dotting the *i* of *Elvis*. And in smaller letters underneath: "world's largest . . . COLLECTION"; a collection of what, it did not say. But underneath that was the name of the place, and the reason I'd stopped. The Elvis Presley Heartbreak Motel.

There had been no billboards dispensing advance word of this.

The Heartbreak Motel was U-shaped and vaguely Alpine in its architecture, with a bush-filled courtyard in the middle and the Elvis Museum at the base of the U. Out front a wooden facsimile of a street sign read ELVIS PRESLEY BLVD., referring, as near as I could figure, to the parking lot. A 1955 yellow-and-black Cadillac was parked beside the street sign, so I gripped its fins and posed for a picture.

Just inside the door to the museum was a giftshop full of Elvis souvenirs and a tired-looking woman behind a counter that served as motel registration desk, giftshop cash register and museum ticket booth. The "museum" was the room directly behind her.

Bob picked up a foot-long cylinder of hard candy that spelled, of course, "Elvis." There was a sticker on the cellophane that covered the candy, and Bob read it aloud. "'Elvis's name goes all the way through the candy.'" He laughed. "Wonder if it really does."

"It really does," the woman said, nodding. "The other day we ate a piece just to see." A garish painting of Elvis grinned at us over her right shoulder, a dull gold chain taped to his neck. I doubt I'd have known it was Elvis had we not been at the Heartbreak Motel.

We walked around, doing what tourists are supposed to do in giftshops: picking things up, showing them to each another, trying on silly hats, moving all the moving parts of elaborate gee-gaws, all with no intention of spending any money. This is free entertainment, and only the most insufferable highbrow could deny the pleasure to be had in running one's hands through a box of rubber jumping frogs with Elvis tattoos on their bellies.

From what we could see in the giftshop and through a gap in the curtain to the back room, we decided the museum wasn't worth the $4 admission. Most of the memorabilia had belonged not to Elvis but to J. D. Sumner, the guitar player during Presley's Vegas years. There looked to be a lot of pictures of J. D. and Elvis together, J. D. in cowboy shirts and bolo ties, Elvis in tinted glasses and capes of incessant rhinestones.

On our way out Bob turned, walked up to the desk and, pointing past the woman, asked, "I'm curious. Is that a commissioned portrait of Elvis over there, or is it just someone who admired him?"

I couldn't tell if she noticed Bob's patronizing tone.

"I'm not really sure," she said. "It's not the orig'nal oll, and we kept saying, 'That can't be Elvis Presley, it doesn't look like Elvis Presley.' But we found out it's been done from an actual photograph."

"An actual photograph, huh?" Bob said. "It looks a little like Robert Goulet."

The woman smiled. "The orig'nal oll of this painting is hanging on the wall in Graceland Mansion."

Arkansas may be the most forgotten state in the Union (North Dakota would give it more competition if it weren't part of a North/South pairing). It's certainly not a state you just stumble on, unless you're going cross-country on Interstate 40. Here's a look at the sort of tourists who actually seek Arkansas out . . . or find themselves there by mistake.

Charles Allbright
Tourists: Weird, But Nice 1986

A SCHOLARLY APPEARING MAN walks into the state-operated tourist information center at Corning, in far northeast Arkansas, looking for want he calls historic cemetery information.

"Yes sir, we'll do the best we can," the Arkansas greeter says.

"What I'm trying to find," the visitor says, "is the grave of the horse my grandfather rode down here during the Civil War."

Mark up one failure, a rare one, for the Corning tourist information center.

Down in the far southwest, a woman is jerked through the door of the Texarkana tourist center by a dog on a leash.

"Is there a place where I can water my dog?" she asks, her voice edged with urgency.

The information specialist says, "We don't have actual watering bowls, but there's a nice fountain out there where he can get a drink."

The visitor is jerked back out through the door, shouting, "That's not the kind of watering I'm talking about!"

Mark one up for education at the Texarkana tourist center.

Up at Bentonville, near the Missouri line, a man strides into the tourist information center wearing a big, friendly smile and nothing else but a pair of droopy boxer shorts.

"Yes sir!" the Arkansas hostess blurts. She lurches half out of her chair, sees the shorts are held together with a giant safety pin, and locks eyes desperately with the approaching tourist.

He says something with a foreign accent.

"Sir! How's that sir?"

Now they are separated only by the counter, which is

both good and bad—he's mighty close, but at least you can't see his underwear.

It turned out that the visitor couldn't have been nicer. The center hostess explained to us:

"He was from Holland, and he just didn't understand what kind of shorts American men wear on vacation. I mean, to this man a pair of shorts was a pair of shorts."

At the Governor's Conference on Tourism here, we sat in after hours while a room full of prettily uniformed hostesses let their hair down and told about their experiences at Arkansas's border information stations.

The consensus was that most of the thousands of tourists who come to Arkansas annually couldn't be nicer; also that a few of them couldn't be weirder.

"We have this one regular visitor," one of the girls said, "who if you take your eyes off him, he'll drop down on the floor and start doing pushups, that or walking around on his hands. Except for that, he's a very nice and conservative gentleman."

Being a hostess for the State of Arkansas, the specialist is supposed to keep her cool. Especially when a visitor expresses amazement that she is wearing shoes, or asks where the hillbillies are, or wonders which way to the moonshine.

"How long did you have to practice to learn to talk like that?" a visitor asks.

But the funny folks are not the problems.

"The one you dread is the man who comes in with a map all opened up. He doesn't know where he is, where he's been, or where he's going. You're supposed to straighten him out, and the map is probably of South Carolina."

By the tourists themselves, the Arkansas centers are rated among the country's very best, meaning the friendliest and most helpful. One way or another, the greeters come up with information about farming, local taxes, day after tomorrow's temperature at Pocatello, Idaho, and New Jersey telephone exchanges.

Some things are stumpers, though, like horses' burial

grounds, and the kind of telephone call that came in long distance to one of the border centers.

"How far am I from Little Rock?" a distressed female caller said.

"Where are you calling from now?" the information specialist asked.

"I don't know," the woman said.

New Orleans has a special appeal, in that a visit there is like leaving the United States, yet it is the home of much that is special in America, from jazz and strip-joints to creole cooking and the pilgrimage to Mardi Gras. Although Americans might consider it a place to unwind and let your hair down, French writer Simone de Beauvoir found it very much a part of puritanical America.

Simone de Beauvoir
Charged With Morality 1953

THE BAND STOPPED PLAYING. A beautiful young woman with raven hair walked onto the platform; she began to dance and take off her clothes slowly, following the prescribed rites of burlesque. From a corner a middle-aged woman watched her indifferently: it was the girl's mother. We heard that the dancer was of good family, had studied much, and was intelligent and cultured; but in New Orleans, strippers are readily surrounded by legendary auras. This girl, however, was beautiful and attractive. The more she took off, the more forbidding grew the looks around her; they expressed detached curiosity, polite but bored; when she abandoned her panties, keeping only the "patch"—a spangled triangle held by a silken thread—the atmosphere was so charged with morality that one might have been in church.

Translated from the French by Patrick Dudley

Most of Florida is not quite part of the South. The southern part of the state is a strange conjunction of Northern retirees and vacationers and Caribbean emigrés.

Whatever it is, especially with the founding of Disney World, it is the major tourist destination of Americans and foreigners alike. But before we rush on to southern Florida, Ring Lardner has a short report to make on the Southern town of St. Augustine. Then he continues on to old Palm Beach, the resort that has always worked hard to stay a hundred years behind, and a couple classes ahead, of the times. But life goes on in the midst of what Palm Beach tries to be, and the eagle eyes of American travel humorist Ludwig Bemelmans catches it at a glance. Then, classic American humorist James Thurber travels all the way down to the Florida Keys to talk to the most isolated man in America about the few tourists that have come his way.

Ring Lardner
The Oldest Around 1917

FIRST, WE WENT TO ST. GEORGE STREET and visited the oldest house in the United States. Then we went to Hospital Street and seen the oldest house in the United States. Then we turned the corner and went down St. Francis Street and inspected the oldest house in the United States. Then we dropped into a soda fountain and I had an egg phosphate, made from the oldest egg in the Western Hemisphere. We passed up lunch and got into a carriage drawn by the oldest horse in Florida, and we rode through the country all afternoon and the driver told us some o' the oldest jokes in the book. He felt it was only fair to give his customers a good time when he was chargin' a dollar an hour, and he had his gags rehearsed so's he could tell the same one a thousand times and never change a word. And the horse knowed where the point come in every one and stopped to laugh.

Ring Lardner
Bathin' in Palm Beach 1917

AFTER BREAKFAST we went to the room for a change o' raiment. I put on my white trousers and wished to heaven that the sun'd go under a cloud till I got used to tellin' people without words just where my linen began and I left off. The rest o' my outfit was white shoes that hurt, and white sox, and a two-dollar silk shirt that showed up a zebra, and a red tie and a soft collar and a blue coat. The Missus wore a sport suit that I won't try to describe—you'll probably see it on her sometime in the next five years.

We went down-stairs again and out on the porch, where some o' the old birds was takin' a sun bath.

"Where now?" I says.

"The beach, o' course," says the Missus.

"Where is it at?" I ast her.

"I suppose," she says, "that we'll find it somewheres near the ocean."

"I don't believe you can stand this climate," says I.

"The ocean," she says, "must be down at the end o' that avenue, where most everybody seems to be headed."

"Havin' went to our room and back twice, I don't feel like another five-mile hike," I says.

"It ain't no five miles," she says; "but let's ride, anyway."

"Come on," says I, pointin' to a street-car that was standin' in the middle o' the avenue.

"Oh, no," she says. "I've watched and found out that the real people takes them funny-lookin' wheel chairs."

I was wonderin' what she meant when one o' them pretty near run over us. It was part bicycle, part go-cart and part African. In the one we dodged they was room for one passenger, but some o' them carried two.

"I wonder what they'd soak us for the trip," I says.

"Not more'n a dime, I don't believe," says the Missus.

But when we'd hired one and been w'isked down under the palms and past the golf field to the bath-house, we was obliged to part with fifty cents legal and tender.

"I feel much refreshed," I says. "I believe when it comes time to go back I'll be able to walk."

The bath-house is acrost the street from the other hotel, the Breakers, that the man had told us was full for the season. Both buildin's fronts on the ocean; and, boy, it's some ocean! I bet they's fish in there that never seen each other!

"Oh, let's go bathin' right away!" says the Missus.

"Our suits is up to the other beanery," says I, and I was glad of it. They wasn't nothin' temptin' to me about them man-eatin' waves.

But the Wife's a persistent cuss.

"We won't go to-day," she says, "but we'll go in the bath-house and get some rooms for to-morrow."

The bath-house porch was a ringer for the *Follies*. Here and down on the beach was where you seen the costumes at this time o'day. I was so busy rubberin' that I passed the entrance door three times without noticin' it. From the top o' their heads to the bottom o' their feet the girls was a mess o' colors. They wasn't no two dressed alike and if any one o' them had of walked down State Street we'd of had an epidemic o' stiff neck to contend with in Chi. Finally the Missus grabbed me and hauled me into the office.

"Two private rooms," she says to the clerk. "One lady and one gent."

"Five dollars a week apiece," he says. "But we're all filled up."

"You ought to be all locked up!" I says.

"Will you have anything open to-morrow?" ast the Missus.

"I think I can fix you then," he says.

"What do we get for the five?" I ast him.

"Private room and we take care o' your bathin' suit," says he.

"How much if you don't take care o' the suit?" I ast him. "My suit's been gettin' along fine with very little care."

"Five dollars a week apiece," he says, "and if you want the rooms you better take 'em, because they're in big demand."

By the time we'd closed this grand bargain, everybody'd moved offen the porch and down to the water, where a couple dozen o' them went in for a swim and the rest set and watched. They was a long row o' chairs on the beach for spectators and we was just goin' to flop into two o' them when another bandit come up and told us it'd cost a dime apiece per hour.

"We're goin' to be here two weeks," I says. "Will you sell us two chairs?"

He wasn't in no comical mood, so we sunk down on the sand and seen the show from there. We had plenty o' company that preferred these kind o' seats free to the chairs at ten cents a whack.

Besides the people that was in the water gettin' knocked down by the waves and pretendin' like they enjoyed it, about half o' the gang on the sand was wearin' bathin' suits just to be clubby. You could tell by lookin' at the suits that they hadn't never been wet and wasn't intended for no such ridic'lous purpose. I wisht I could describe 'em to you, but it'd take a female to do it right.

One little girl, either fourteen or twenty-four, had white silk slippers and sox that come pretty near up to her ankles, and from there to her knees it was just plain Nature. Northbound from her knees was a pair o' bicycle trousers that disappeared when they come to the bottom of her Mother Hubbard. This here garment was a thing without no neck or sleeves that begin bulgin' at the top and spread out gradual all the way down, like a croquette. To top her off, she had a jockey cap; and—believe me—I'd of played her mount acrost the board. They was plenty o'class in the field with her, but nothin' that approached her speed. Later on I seen her several times round the hotel, wearin' somethin' near the same outfit, without the jockey cap and with longer croquettes.

We set there in the sand till people begun to get up and leave. Then we trailed along back o' them to the Breakers' porch, where they was music to dance and stuff to inhale.

"We'll grab a table," I says to the Missus. "I'm dyin' o' thirst."

But I was allowed to keep on dyin'.

"I can serve you somethin' soft," says the waiter.

"I'll bet you can't!" I says.

"You ain't got no locker here?" he says.

"What do you mean—locker?" I ast him.

"It's the locker liquor law," he says. "We can serve you a drink if you own your own bottles."

"I'd just as soon own a bottle," I says. "I'll become the proprietor of a bottle o' beer."

"It'll take three or four hours to get it for you," he says, "and you'd have to order it through the order desk. If you're stoppin' at one o' the hotels and want a drink once in a w'ile, you better get busy and put in an order."

So I had to watch the Missus put away a glass of orange juice that cost forty cents and was just the same size as they give us for breakfast free for nothin'. And, not havin' had nothin' to make me forget that my feet hurt, I was obliged to pay another four bits for an Afromobile to cart us back to our own boardin' house. * * *

The next day we went to the ocean at the legal hour— half past eleven. I never had so much fun in my life. The surf was runnin' high, I heard 'em say; and I don't know which I'd rather do, go bathin' in the ocean at Palm Beach when the surf is runnin' high, or have a dentist get one o' my molars ready for a big inlay at a big outlay. Once in a w'ile I managed to not get throwed on my head when a wave hit me. As for swimmin', you had just as much chance as if you was at State and Madison at the noon hour. And

161

before I'd been in a minute they was enough salt in my different features to keep the Blackstone hotel runnin' all through the onion season.

The Missus enjoyed it just as much as me. She tried to pretend at first, and when she got floored she'd give a squeal that was supposed to mean heavenly bliss. But after she'd been bruised from head to feet and her hair looked and felt like spinach with French dressin', and she'd drank all she could hold o' the Gulf Stream, she didn't resist none when I drug her in to shore and staggered with her up to our private rooms at five a week per each.

Without consultin' her, I went to the desk at the Casino and told 'em they could have them rooms back.

"All right," says the clerk, and turned our keys over to the next in line.

"How about a refund?" I ast him; but he was waitin' on somebody else.

After that we done our bathin' in the tub. But we was down to the beach every morning at eleven-thirty to watch the rest o' them get batted round.

Ludwig Bemelmans
An Unforgettable Picture 1942

MIAMI IS MIAMI, and by no other name is there a city such as this. The hotel employees were as efficient and quick as dentists, and fingerprinted besides. Everything is to be had here from caviar to a Goodyear blimp. From a point of design and efficiency the new hotels in Miami Beach are motels.

The main highway to Palm Beach was now an unending, open-all-night string of tourist cabins, orange and papaya juice pavilions, sea shells, carved coconuts, and cypress-knee souvenir stands. There is another, quiet road along the ocean, one of the finest drives in the world.

An unforgettable picture presented itself to me at a turn

in that road. It was past the S curve that leads to the Hutton castle in Palm Beach. This edifice always reminds me of an advertisement for breakfast food. I am certain that at night gnomes work there under the stairs of the baronial halls and in the vaulted cellars wrapping crunchy crackies, full of golden goodness, into bright packages and mailing them out in Josef Urban boxes.

The castle's garden faces the unceasing sound of the waves; the moon shone through the long, thin fins of palm leaves, and on a bulkhead near the sea sat a black gardener and a maid, engaged in ardent courtship. Beyond them, two tugs tried to get a steamer off a sandbank.

James Thurber
Casuals of the Keys 1935

IF YOU KNOW the more remote little islands off the Florida coast, you may have met—although I greatly doubt it—Captain Darke. Darrell Darke. His haunted key is, for this reason and that, the most inaccessible of them all. I came upon it quite by chance and doubt that I could find it again. I saw him first that moment when my shining little launch, so impudently summer-resortish, pushed its nose against the lonely pier on which he stood. Tall, dark, melancholy, his white shirt open at the throat, he reminded me instantly of that other solitary wanderer among forgotten islands, the doomed Lord Jim.

I stepped off the boat and he came toward me with a lean brown hand out-thrust. "I'm Darke," he said, simply, "Darrell Darke." I shook hands with him. He seemed pleased to encounter someone from the outside world. I found out later that no white man had set foot on his remote little key for several years.

He took me to a little thatched hut and waved me to a bamboo chair. It was a pleasant place, with a bed of dried palm leaves, a few withered books, some fishing equipment, and a bright rifle. Darke produced from somewhere a bottle with a greenish heavy liquid in it, and two glasses. "Opono," he said, apologetically. "Made from the sap of the opono tree. Horrible stuff, but kicky." I asked him if he would care for a touch of Bacardi, of which I had a quart on the launch, and he said he would. I went down and got it.

"A newspaperman, eh?" said Darke, with interest, as I filled up the glasses for the third time. "You must meet a lot of interesting people." I really felt that I had met a lot of interesting people and, under slight coaxing, began to tell about them: Gene Tunney, Eddie Rickenbacker, the Grand Duchess Marie, William Gibbs McAdoo. Darke listened to my stories with quick attention, thirsty as he was for news of the colorful civilization which, he told me, he had put behind him twenty years before.

"You must," I said at last, to be polite, "have met some interesting people yourself."

"No," he said. "All of a stripe, until you came along. Last chap that put in here, for example, was a little fellow name of Mark Menafee who turned up one day some three years ago in an outboard motor. He was only a trainer of fugitives from justice." Darke reached for the glass I had filled again.

"I never heard of anyone being that," I said. "What did he do?"

"He coached fugitives from justice," said Darke. "Seems Menafee could spot one instantly. Take the case of Burt Fredericks he told me about. Fredericks was a bank defaulter from Connecticut. Menafee spotted him on a Havana boat—knew him from his pictures in the papers. 'Hello, Burt,' says Menafee, casually. Fredericks whirled around. Then he caught himself and stared blankly at Menafee. 'My name is Charles Brandon,' he says. Menafee won his confidence and for a fee and his expenses engaged to coach Fredericks not to be caught off his guard and answer to the name of Burt. He'd shadow Fredericks from city to city, contriving to come upon him unexpectedly in dining-rooms, men's lounges, bars, and crowded hotel lobbies. 'Why Burt!' Menafee would say, gaily, or 'It's old Fredericks!' like someone meeting an old friend after years. Fredericks got so he never let on—unless he was addressed as Charlie or Brandon. Far as I know he was never caught. Menafee made enough to keep going, coaching fugitives, but it was a dullish kind of job." Darke fell silent. I sat watching him.

"Did you ever meet any other uninteresting people?" I asked.

"There was Harrison Cammery," said Darke, after a moment. "He put in here one night in a storm, dressed in full evening clothes. Came from New York—I don't know how. There never was a sign of a boat or anything to show how he got here. He was always that way while he was here, dully incomprehensible. He had the most uninteresting of manias, which is monomania. He was a goldfish-holder." Darke stopped and seemed inclined to let the story end there.

"What do you mean, a goldfish-holder?" I demanded.

"Cammery had been a professional billard-player," said Darke. "He told me that the strain of developing absolutely nerveless hands finally told on him. He had trained so that he could balance five BB shot on the back of each of his fingers indefinitely. One night, at a party where the host had a bowl of goldfish, the guests got to trying to catch them with one grab of their hand. Nobody could do it until Cammery tried. He caught up one of the fish and held it lightly in his closed hand. He told me that the wettish fluttering of that fish against the palm of his hand became a thing he couldn't forget. He got to snatching up goldfish and holding them, wherever he went. At length he had to have a bowl of them beside the table when he played his billiard matches, and would hold one between innings the way tennis-players take a mouthful of water. The effect finally was to destroy his muscular precision, so he took to the islands. One day he was gone from here—I don't know how. I was glad enough. A singularly one-track and boring fellow."

"Who else has put in here?" I asked, filling them up again.

"Early in 1913," said Darke, after a pause in which he seemed to make an effort to recall what he was after, "early in 1913 an old fellow with a white beard—must have been seventy-five or eighty—walked into this hut one day. He was dripping wet. Said he swam over from the mainland and he probably did. It's fifty miles. Lots of boats can be had for the taking along the main coast, but this fellow was apparently too stupid to take one. He was as dull about everything as about that. Used to recite short stories word for word—said he wrote them himself. He was a writer like you, but he didn't seem to have met any interesting people. Talked only about himself, where he'd come from, what he'd done. I didn't pay any attention to him. I was glad when, one night, he disappeared. His name was. . ." Darke put his head back and stared at the roof of his hut, striving to remember. "Oh, yes," he said. "His name was Bierce. Ambrose Bierce."

"You say that was in 1913, early in 1913?" I asked, excitedly.

"Yes, I'm sure of it," said Darke, "because it was the same year C-18769 showed up here."

"Who was C-18769?" I asked.

"It was a carrier pigeon," said Darke. "Flew in here one night tuckered by the trip from the mainland, and flopped down on that bed with its beak open, panting hard. It was red-eyed and dishevelled. I noticed it had something sizable strapped under its belly and I saw its registration number, on a silver band fastened to its leg: C-18769. When it got rested up it hung around here for quite a while. I didn't pay much attention to it. In those days I used to get the New York papers about once a month off a supply boat that used to put in at an island ten miles from here. I'd row over. One day I saw a notice in one of the papers about this bird. Some concern or other, for a publicity stunt, had arranged to have this bird carry a thousand dollars in hundred-dollar bills from the concern's offices to the place where the bird homed, some five hundred miles away. The bird never got there. The papers had all kinds of theories: the bird had been shot and robbed, it had fallen in the water and drowned, or it had got lost."

"The last was right," I said. "It must have got lost."

"Lost, hell," said Darke. "After I read the stories I caught it up one day, suddenly, and examined the packet strapped to it. It only had four hundred and sixty-five dollars left."

I felt a little weak. Finally, in a small voice, I asked: "Did you turn it over to the authorities?"

"Certainly not," said Darrell Darke. "A man or a bird's life is his own to lead, down here. I simply figured this pigeon for a fool, and let him go. What could he do, after the money was gone? Nothing." Darke rolled and lighted a cigarette and smoked a while, silently. "That's the kind of beings you meet with down here," he said. "Stupid, dullish, lacking in common sense, fiddling along aimlessly. Menafee, Cammery, Bierce, C-18769—all the same. It gets monotonous. Tell me more about this Grand Duchess Marie. She must be a most interesting person."

Alligator Hunt
Jacques Le Moyne de Morgues, 1591.

"Whatever happened to all the amber waves of grain?"

❧The Midwest

❧*Americans are like kids on a bus: when something happens, they all flock to one side to see, and almost tip the bus over. With America, it's the coasts. Most people used to live on the east coast, with only the hardy (and often greedy) souls taking their wagons and trains out West. Now everyone's picking up from the East Coast and flying West, where it's happening, as fast as they can.*

Foreigners are like that, too. There's so much America between the coasts, it's hard to decide where to start. So most foreigners don't bother, unless they've got business. New York, Washington, Orlando, Los Angeles, and San Francisco seem to do the trick. But there are even hardy souls among foreign travelers, who insist on seeing not only the Grand Canyon and Las Vegas, but even the Midwest. And there are also some American tourists who've seen everything, and the Plains are all that's left. Ah, that black soil, those ultra-safe highways without a single curve, and all those nice people, so happy to see their first tourist since the soy crop failed.

To introduce us to the Midwest, we have a few words from Punch's *Alex Atkinson, the hard-to-satisfy Charles Dickens, and John Steinbeck. Then British travel writer Jonathan Raban goes up in the Arch at St. Louis.*

Alex Atkinson
Splendid Isolation 1959

I AM BOUND TO SAY that at the outset the Middle West was something of a disappointment to me, because it turned out to be in the north.

To make matters worse, according to my calculations it lies a little to the east and quite a distance from the middle, which is in Kansas—or was, until Alaska threw everything into confusion. (Of course, there are inhabitants of Kansas who claim they're Middle West anyway, but you'll *always* find people who want to get in on the act, and it shouldn't be encouraged. Once you admit Kansas, before you know where you are you'll have New Mexico hammering at the door, and the thing will become farcical.)

On the whole I believe it would be more accurate to call the Middle West the Middle East, if anything, and I suggested this to a man in Oshkosh. He went on manufacturing truck axles for a few minutes and then he said, "That don't alter the fact that Edna Ferber was born in Wisconsin." You can't argue with men in Oshkosh, and that also goes for men in Lawrenceburg, Indiana, where they make buggies for Hollywood. ("Why are you making all these buggies, neighbour?" I asked this man in Lawrenceburg. "For Hollywood," said the man. "Do they use a lot of buggies, then, in Hollywood?" I asked. "I don't know what they do with them," said the man, "but they sure seem crazy about 'em, and that's good enough for me.")

Dust-stained, smelling of hot rubber and sheep-dip, with alfalfa seeds in my hair and my convertible ankle-deep in peanut-shells, I reached the Middle West after driving for about three weeks in a dead straight line along a highway, stopping only for gas, water, hot-dogs, gophers, highway patrols, road-blocks, landslides, stick-ups, floods, free air and unfenced cattle. It is a region of contrasts: in one Main

Street you might see a boy wearing baseball boots and a space-helmet, while in another you might not. Chances are you will, though. It is also a region of isolationism, because its people are trapped. On the whole they don't complain about this, but the fact remains that they are hemmed in, probably for ever—by a lot of lakes and the Dominion of Canada to the north, by the Rockies to the west, by the Alleghenies to the east, and by the hill-billies to the south. (Some reckless spirits have in the past tried to pioneer an escape route down through Kentucky, only to find themselves nailed to barn-doors or held captive in the mountains and worshipped as mysterious ju-ju men.) To many Midwesterners, therefore, the outside world remains an enigma, and a pretty mixed-up one at that. They regard Charleston as just an old-time dance, Lebanon as simply a town in either Indiana or Missouri. Lebanon means nothing more to them: they don't know about Lebanon Oregon, Lebanon Penn., Lebanon Vermont, or even Lebanon Tennessee. And in a little place in Minnesota I didn't cause the slightest ripple of excitement when I put down my nationality as Zulu in the hotel register. The hotel clerk was the only one who showed any interest. He asked me if we were still pestered with kangaroos in China, and told the chef to rustle up some astrakhan for my supper. To give them their due, however, I found that many Midwesterners know about England. England is where the British live. The British roam around constantly in their gunboats colonizing defenceless people. They are chiefly remarkable in that they flatly refuse to pay their War Debts.

A maker of steel wagon beds near Chillicothe, Missouri, where Sloan's Liniment was invented in 1870, told me that a good many Midwesterners wouldn't have picked the Middle West as a place to live if they'd had a choice. "The way I figure it," he said, "it all came about by accident. In the old days most everybody from the east was heading out to California, and it just so happened that round about half-way they hit the Middle West, and a lot of wagons broke

171

down. So some folks said 'The hell with it, we ain't in no fit condition to do a repair job on this here old wagon, we might as well stay right here.' And they did. So they became our ancestors, and if it hadn't been for that this whole place might still be Cherokee country to-day, same as Oklahoma, and I ain't saying it wouldn't have been an improvement, at that."

He was being modest, of course, for there are splendid things to see in the Middle West, what with wall-eyed pike in the Ozarks, the University of Minnesota, the grave of War Eagle, the Home of ex-President Truman, and one hundred and forty varieties of hybrid lilacs in the Nichols Arboretum, Ann Arbour, Michigan (free, open daily 9 to 9). There is also Ohio, if it comes to that, where they make soap, tables, false teeth, wine and playing-cards, and where, in the town of Tiffin, Heidelberg College was founded in 1850. Ohio is also notorious for the number of presidents it has produced. There were seven in all, and they were all Republicans. Two were shot dead, and one was Warren G. Harding. There are more Methodists in Columbus than you'd think possible, and I met a girl student at Ohio State University who was taking courses in Old Provençal and Ice Cream Manufacturing.

I spent enough time in a typical small Midwestern town to be able to form a vivid impression of the place. It has a population of nearly four thousand, of whom a hundred and fifty are dentists. It lies in the midst of a vast, empty plain: you could tear south down the highway some evening at eighty miles an hour (in your convertible) and it would be no more than a flurry of lights as you passed it, or a snatch of Frank Sinatra on a juke-box. On Main Street there are four pediatricians, five drug-stores, three morticians, one chainstore, one corn chandler's, four churches, a temple, two super-markets, two movie theatres, five bars, three used-car marts, two banks and a wooden Indian. This is the centre of the town, and the gaily coloured convertibles make a pleasant sight parked four deep at each side of the street while the people who are gradually paying for them go about their business or pleasure on every hand. Here are fashionable matrons trudging along to rest their feet in beauty parlours after a hard morning entertaining some visiting celebrity at a pre-lecture *soirée* (ninety-seven guests in their very best rhinestones, plus one husband to mix the drinks). Here are two corpulent, beringed gentlemen with hula girls painted gaily on their ties. They are fanning themselves with their sharkskin trilbies as they pause for a democratic chat with a humble newsvendor under the plane trees. They are running for mayor, and so is he. Here is a bunch of kids, swinging along happily from the nearest vacant lot with bats, balls, gloves, and gum, singing some quaint American folk-song as they turn in to the Happi Phun Parlor to play the fruit machines before going home to television. Here is another bunch, thundering down the street like bats out of hell in their sawn-off hot-rods, scattering the quick and the dead. Here is another bunch, in black leather jackets slightly old-fashioned by New York standards, shuffling menacingly up the street with their hands in their pockets and their faces pudgy, eyeless, identical. Are they on their way to a lynching? To dancing-class? To finish their homework? There is no way of telling. Here is the man who runs the town, tossing away half a cigar as he elbows aside the shirt-sleeved cop on the corner and strolls into a barber-shop to investigate some discrepancy in last week's taking on the horses. Here is the editor of the local paper, hurrying out of his office wearing a green eye-shade, to snatch a hasty ham on rye with dill pickle, ketchup and mustard before finishing his fearless leading article on graft in the sanitation department. Altogether it makes a lazy, comfortable picture in the sunlight—a shining example to the underdeveloped nations of the world.

Charles Dickens
Plain Prairie 1842

NOW, A PRAIRIE is undoubtedly worth seeing—but more, that one may say one has seen it, than for any sublimity it possesses in itself. Like most things, great or small, in this country, you hear of it with considerable exaggerations. Basil Hall was really quite right in depreciating the general character of the scenery. The widely-famed Far West is not to be compared with even the tamest portions of Scotland or Wales. You stand upon the prairie, and see the unbroken horizon all round you. You are on a great plain, which is like a sea without water. I am exceedingly fond of wild and lonely scenery, and believe that I have the faculty of being as much impressed by it as any man living. But the prairie fell, by far, short of my preconceived idea. I felt no such emotions as I do in crossing Salisbury plain. The excessive flatness of the scene makes it dreary, but tame. Grandeur is certainly not its characteristic. I retired from the rest of the party, to understand my own feelings the better; and looked all round, again and again. It was fine. It was worth the ride. The sun was going down, very red and bright; and the prospect looked like that ruddy sketch of Catlin's, which attracted our attention (you remember?); except that there was not so much ground as he represents, between the spectator and the horizon. But to say (as the fashion is, here) that the sight is a landmark in one's existence, and awakens a new set of sensations, is sheer gammon. I would say to every man who can't see a prairie—go to Salisbury plain, Marlborough downs, or any of the broad, high, open lands near the sea. Many of them are fully as impressive; and Salisbury plain is *decidedly* more so.

John Steinbeck
What It Was Like 1962

'LL TELL YOU WHAT IT WAS LIKE. Go to the Ufizzi in Florence, the Louvre in Paris, and you are so crushed with the numbers, once the might of greatness, that you go away distressed, with a feeling like constipation. And then when you are alone and remembering, the canvases sort themselves out; some are eliminated by your taste or your limitations, but others stand up clear and clean. Then you can go back to look at one thing untroubled by the shouts of the multitude. After confusion I can go into the Prado in Madrid and pass unseeing the thousand pictures shouting for my attention and I can visit a friend—a not large Greco, *San Pablo con un Libro*. St. Paul has just closed the book. His finger marks the last page read and on his face are the wonder and will to understand after the book is closed. Maybe understanding is possible only after. Years ago when I used to work in the woods it was said of lumber men that they did their logging in the whorehouse and their sex in the woods. So I have to find my way through the exploding production lines of the Middle West while sitting alone beside a lake in northern Michigan.

Jonathan Raban
Helpless With Laughter 1981

OBEDIENTLY, as if I had swallowed my dose of Lithium and were following the instructions of the head nurse, I had ridden to the top of the Arch. * * *

We were cranked up to the top of the Arch in a train of tiny vandalized cars. I was squashed opposite a woman from Sacramento. Since the size of the car forced us to interlock our legs, it seemed natural enough to talk on the bumpy journey up through the dark.

She said: "The Arch is supposed to be to St. Louis what the Eiffel Tower is to Paris." She sounded like a tour guide. We gained another stair in the blackness with a terrific rattle and clank.

"Say that again?"

"The Arch is. . ." There was a sniff, and she started again. "The Arch is supposed to be to St. Louis what the Eiffel. . ." But she couldn't manage it. She was helpless with giggles. I tried to say it, and nearly reached the word "Paris" before something broke in my solar plexus. There were five people in the car. By the time we were three-quarters of the way up, we were all trying to get the sentence out and falling, helpless with laughter, into one another's laps. We tried to say it in chorus. I suggested that it might be easier if we sang it. When we reached the top, we were gurgling like maniacs. On the viewing platform, people shrank from contact with anyone from our car, and we in our turn shrank from each other. When I tried to grin at the woman who had started this riot of happy hysteria, she refused to catch my eye.

To ease us into the West, Philip Hamburger passes through the Missouri town of St. Joseph, home of the infamous outlaw Jesse James, and tells how it feels to live in a town known for having harbored an outlaw.

Philip Hamburger
Stuck With Jesse James 1965

THERE IS NO NEED TO BE FRIGHTENED by the man who shows visitors through the house in which Jesse James was killed. He just *looks* tough. He works day in and day out amidst memorabilia of the great outlaw, and this tends to surround him with an aura of cold steel, midnight raids, and train robberies. Actually, he is as harmless as his "lecture," and parents who protectively clasp their children to them as they move from room to room would be well advised to relax. Nothing untoward will happen. Jesse James is not outside, loading his Colt. He is hatching no stickup. He is as dead as a mackerel. He has been dead since April 3, 1882, when, living in St. Joseph under the name of Thomas Howard, he was shot in the back by Robert Ford—"the dirty little coward," in the words of the old song, "that shot Mr. Howard." At the time of the shooting, the house stood at Thirteenth and Lafayette, near St. Paul's Lutheran Church. It stood there until 1940, when its owner, feeling that he owed it to the American public to make the house more accessible, set it down a few miles out of town, on Route 71, a major artery between St. Joseph and Kansas City, sixty miles south. Whole families had been whizzing through St. Joseph without taking advantage of the educational opportunities offered by a visit to the house. Today, it rests next to Jesse James Super Service (a gas station) and the Jesse James Motel ("Ultra Modern"). The scholarly and historical tone is firmly established by a sign outside reading "MURDER! JESSE JAMES KILLED HERE!"

Inside, the guide, whose pants are unpressed, collects fifty cents from each visitor and delivers his lecture in a low, semi-dramatic mumble. In order to catch all the historical nuances, one must listen carefully. The guide's lecture is memorized, and does not vary from tour to tour. He points to a dusty cabinet. "Within resides the Bible of Mrs. James," he says. "Guns and nails and his grandfather's shoes, likewise the key-wind Waltham, the very one was on him when he was killed. His mother's specs. Just one piece of the chair left there from the chair on which he fell back dead, whole rest of the chair tore all to pieces by hordes, next room please." A sampler on the wall of the next room reads, "God Bless Our Home." A hole in the wall the size of a barn door is covered with glass. "Jesse was standing on the chair which was tore all to pieces when he was shot in the back by Bob Ford, who was itching for the reward money, went in the right ear and out the left eye, note the bullet hole in the wall beneath glass as protection against hordes, April 3, 1882, next room please. Bed where they laid the dead man, don't find many quilts made like that nowadays, April 3, 1882, next room please. Within resides the Bible of Mrs. James. Guns and nails and his grandfather's shoes, likewise the key-wind Waltham, the very one. . ." Visitors often tiptoe out, suspecting that the historian has been carried away by his material. On the way, many stop to admire a quotation, framed and hung on the wall: "I like to see a man proud of the place in which he lives. I like to see a man live so that his place will be proud of him. —Abraham Lincoln."

St. Joseph—known to its residents as St. Joe—is stuck with Jesse James, and on the whole would prefer to change the subject. The people of St. Joseph wish he had been shot in the back in Kansas City, or even in the front as long as it happened somewhere else. Every once in a while, somebody turns up with a recollection of having played as a child with Jesse James' old guns in a back yard somewhere in St. Joe, but the mention of his name brings forth mention of matters closer to the hearts of St. Joe people. "Jesse James was a bad boy, all right," a St. Joe resident said not long ago, "but we still make Big Chief writing tablets here at Western Tablet & Stationery."

THE MID-WEST

Arnold Roth. By permission of Punch Publications Ltd.

❧The West

❧More than any other part of the United States, the West is the place people come to know—or to think they know—from watching movies. Cowboys and Indians, barmaids and dancers, horses and cattle, mesas and canyons. Shake well and pour, and you've got yourself a Western.

But humorists have somehow managed to find a lot more West of the Mississippi than these common ingredients. And when they examine one of the ingredients, it looks mighty different than it does on camera. The Grand Canyon looks less grand, the Alamo less memorable, and the geysers at Yellowstone less faithful.

We begin our look at the West with its most amusing denizen: the tumbleweed. On our way West, we stop off at Texas with selections by travel writers T. S. Matthews and Bob Greene, then we go down into the Grand Canyon with the classic American humorist Irvin S. Cobb, pass through Salt Lake City with Mark Twain and A. G. MacDonnell, visit a desert with Mark Twain, and stop off at one of the least visited sights in all of the Southwest, the first nuclear crater in Alamogordo, under the supervision of German writer Robert Jungk. Then we head north with Rudyard Kipling, who takes us hiking through the geysers in Yellowstone National Park and salmon fishing in Oregon.

Julian Street
For the Amusement of Mankind 1914

TUMBLEWEED IS A BUSHY PLANT which grows to a height of perhaps three feet, and has a mass of little twigs and branches which make its shape almost perfectly round. Fortunately for the amusement of mankind, it has a weak stalk, so that, when the plant dries, the wind breaks it off at the bottom, and then proceeds to roll it, over and over, across the land. I well remember the first tumbleweed we saw.

"What on earth is that thing?" cried my companion, suddenly, pointing out through the car window. I looked. Some distance away a strange, buff-colored shape was making a swift, uncanny progress toward the east. It wasn't crawling; it wasn't running; but it was traveling fast, with a rolling, tossing, careening motion, like a barrel half full of whisky, rushing down hill. Now it tilted one way, now another; now it shot swiftly into some slight depression in the plain, but only to come bounding lightly out again, with an air indescribably gay, abandoned and inane.

Soon we saw another and another; they became more and more common as we went along until presently they were rushing everywhere, careering in their maudlin course across the prairie, and piled high against the fences along the railroad's right of way, like great concealing snowdrifts.

We fell in love with tumbleweed and never while it was in sight lost interest in its idiotic evolutions. Excepting only tobacco, it is the greatest weed that grows, and it has the advantage over tobacco that it does no man any harm, but serves only to excite his risibilities. It is the clown of vegetation, and it has the air, as it rolls along, of being conscious of its comicality, like the smart *caniche,* in the dog show, who goes and overturns the basket behind the trainer's back; or the circus clown who runs about with a rolling gait, tripping, turning double and triple somersaults, rising, running on, tripping, falling, and turning over and over again. Who shall say that tumbleweed is useless, since it contributes a rare note of drollery to the tragic desolation of the western plains?

T. S. Matthews
Fishy Beyond Words   1962

"I'M BEGINNING TO BELIEVE," M. said, "that I must be deeply happy and live in the finest city on earth."

"Why?"

"Because I never talk about it. These Texans are fishy beyond words. No sane outsider would be convinced by *anything* they say about Dallas, so who are they trying to convert? Themselves?"

Bob Greene
Remember the Alamo?   1985

I WANTED TO SEE SOMETHING REAL. I had had enough of the Eighties; enough of the disposable and the modern. I wanted to go somewhere that felt . . . different.

I thought about it. In all of the United States, where could I go that promised a change? Where could I go that was unspoiled by the rush of time?

It took me several days to figure it out, but when the answer came it was as clear as daybreak. The Alamo. Of course. The Alamo.

I had never been there, but it had to be perfect. I envisioned the big, legendary old mission standing out by itself on the high desert, the wind whistling over the empty miles, sagebrush bouncing along the plains. The Alamo— where for thirteen days in 1836 Jim Bowie, Davy Crockett, Colonel William Travis, and their brave companions fought off the attack of Santa Anna's Mexican troops. The Alamo—

that was it. Everything else in America might be geared to let a fellow down, but the Alamo remained. I closed my eyes. I could almost see it, standing lonely sentry in the desolate heat.

I caught a midday flight to San Antonio. The trip was smooth; riding to my hotel from the airport, I thought about getting into the south Texas mood. Maybe I'd stop somewhere and have a long-neck bottle of Pearl beer. Honest, full-bodied, robust Pearl.

I looked out the window of the cab. The billboard on the right said TASTES GOOD—ONLY 68 CALORIES—PEARL LIGHT.

At the Hyatt my room overlooked the lobby atrium. It occurred to me that I had no idea how to get to the Alamo. I picked up the telephone book to see if it could give me any guidance.

From the San Antonio telephone directory:

Alamo Accessories Filter Division. Alamo Advertising Specialties Company. Alamo Aligning Service. Alamo AMC Jeep Renault Inc. Alamo Answering Service. Alamo Auto Parts. Alamo Awning. Alamo Bail Bonds. . .

I went downstairs and asked the doorman how I would get out to the Alamo, and if he could arrange transportation for me. I said I'd need a way to get back, too; I didn't want to be stranded out on the desert.

He smiled a curious smile at me.

"Just walk over to the next block," he said. "It's right across from Woolworth's."

"What's right across from Woolworth's?" I said.

"The Alamo," he said.

I walked a block. There, across from Woolworth's, was the Alamo.

It was right downtown. In addition to Woolworth's the edifices that surrounded the Alamo included the H. L. Green Variety Store, the G/M Steak House, the Big Apple unisex jeans store, Maldonado Jewelers, and Texas State Optical.

In front of the Alamo itself was Vasquez's Snow-Kone stand.

Next to Vasquez's Snow-Kone stand was a vending box for *USA Today*.

I entered the Alamo. It was tiny. It felt like a one-room schoolhouse. It was dwarfed by the rest of downtown San Antonio.

My fellow tourists included young women wearing Walkman headsets, and young men carrying tape players the size of suitcases. Most of the visitors wore T-shirts; the printing on the front of the shirts featured promotional slogans for the Incredible Hulk, for "M*A*S*H," for Nike running shoes, for the Men at Work '83 North American Tour. * * *

There was a courtyard outside the Alamo. I ran into a family in the midst of an argument. The son was blasting a song called "Ride Like the Wind" from his tape box; his mother, carrying a camera with faces of Mickey Mouse on the strap, and wearing a T-shirt bearing Elvis's face and the words THE KING LIVES ON, was telling him that he had to keep the tape turned off. * * *

Back inside the Alamo I walked over the flagstone floor and stopped in front of a case that held some of Davy Crockett's personal effects. There was Crockett's beaded buckskin vest with onyx buttons; a lock of his hair; his fork; his bear-hunting knife; his razor; his powder case and shot pouch; and his rifle, "Old Betsy."

I heard a mother saying to her son: "Doesn't look like John Wayne, does it?"

I followed her eyes. She was looking up at a portrait of Crockett, painted from life in 1834 by an artist named John C. Chapman. I found it hard to fault the woman standing next to me; if the truth be told, Davy Crockett—at least based on the evidence of the Chapman painting—looked like a cross between Bob Hope and Abbie Hoffman.

I asked Mrs. Boyd (she was wearing a name tag) of the Daughters of the Republic of Texas if I might speak to someone in charge. Mrs. Boyd had sort of a stunned look on her face; I got the impression that she spent many days inside the Alamo. She directed me to a man named Charles Long, who she said was the Alamo's curator. * * *

He told me that it had been a lengthy fight to keep the Alamo as a shrine. "For a long time, it was used for commercial purposes," he said. "When motion pictures first came along, the first place in San Antonio they were shown was right on the side wall of the Alamo. The promoters sold tickets."

I asked him if that was the most blatant example of the Alamo's commercial use.

"Oh, no," Long said. "Years ago, there used to be a liquor store and a hardware store in the long barracks. And at one time the Alamo was a police station, and then a bank."

I excused myself and walked over to the Alamo's gift shop. A woman in an I'M WITH STUPID T-shirt asked her husband, wearing a CHARLIE DANIELS BAND T-shirt, to buy her a book of Texas recipes. * * *

If the woman who had seen Davy Crockett's portrait had been disappointed by the way he looked, I hoped she had continued her tour of the Alamo. There were two other exhibits that, judging by the size of the crowds, were the most popular on the grounds—and that probably would have pleased her more than the Crockett painting.

One of these exhibits was a picture of Davy Crockett, Jim Bowie, and Colonel Travis fighting off the Mexican hordes. In this picture, Davy Crockett looked much more like John Wayne. This was because Davy Crockett *was* John Wayne; the painting was of Wayne's 1960 movie *The Alamo*. Jim Bowie looked like Richard Widmark (who he in fact was); Colonel Travis looked like Laurence Harvey (likewise). The painting was far more satisfying to the visitors than the actual portrait of Crockett.

But as a crowd pleaser, the painting was nothing compared to an artifact that was displayed inside a glass case. At first the object was puzzling; it looked like a gold director's chair.

Which, in fact, it was. It was John Wayne's Screen Directors Guild Award, which officials of the Alamo displayed along with the genuine Crockett-Bowie-Travis memorabilia. * * *

Late at night, alone in my hotel room, I couldn't sleep. I got up and got dressed; I walked back over to the Alamo.

Now I was the only person on the grounds. The building itself was locked, but bright lights illuminated its limestone front. In the artificial light, something showed up that hadn't been quite so noticeable in the daylight: names—names carved by visitors on the facade of the Alamo. Lil Garrett, J. D. Thomas, Billy Waters; I stood there and moved slowly from one edge of the Alamo to the other, reading the names.

I looked back the other way. There was the Hyatt; there was Woolworth's; there was Texas State Optical. A chill wind had come up; now it seemed very cold at the Alamo. I had a Pocket Flight Guide in my suitcase in my room; I could be out of town by ten the next morning.

THE WEST

Arnold Roth. By permission of Punch Publications Ltd.

Irvin S. Cobb
Going Down   1926

O N THE MORNING OF MY ARRIVAL at the canyon there arrived also a lady from somewhere back East, traveling alone, who undertook to walk down the canyon and back up again the same day. One like her comes about once in so often. This lady had a determined manner and one of those figures that seem to overlap. Just by looking at her you knew that the men folks of her family, on both sides, for several generations back had been what are known as steady providers. Also, instinctively as it were, you gathered that she was prominent in reform movements, uplift waves and clubs generally; she had that air about her.

They argued with her—the guides and others—when, after taking a look into that mighty void, she announced her intention of making the journey up and down Bright Angel Trail afoot; they tried to dissuade her. But, no; this lady was not to be deterred. She stated that she would just stroll down during the forenoon and eat her lunch, and pluck a few wild flowers at Indian Gardens, which she could see very plainly from where she stood, and then in the afternoon she would stroll back.

She outlined the undertaking quite calmly but quite positively. Mountain climbing, she said, was nothing new in her experience; she had done it before—often. She did not realize that, before a layman or a laywoman tackles the Grand Canyon afoot, the person should practice climbing up Mount Washington and sliding down it a few thousand times. And then, through long practice, when he—or she—is able to climb all the way up without panting and slide all the way down without bruising, the candidate, merely reversing the process, is almost ready to do the Grand Canyon trip under leg power. She did not realize this and she would not listen to advice.

Possibly distance deceived her. Except when Captain Hance, the official fictionist of the Grand Canyon, was stretching the truth for the benefit of a trusting tourist, everything out in that Arizona country, by reason of the rarefied atmosphere, seemed much closer than it really was. Possibly she wished to save the money she must spend for a mule and a guide if she did the Bright Angel in the regular way; but where, I maintain—where is the economy of saving a dollar or so when you are going to take a pair of broad, dependable feet, such as this lady owned, and treat them in such a way that they are never again the same feet they were?

Possibly she wished to show her independence of the entire male sex. At that, she might have had a lady mule to ride; there were plenty of mules belonging to the gentler sex in the hotel corral. She had a lunch packed up and put on her walking skirt, and she adjusted her glasses and started down alone and afoot and very confident.

We started, too, but on muleback and in another direction. I was riding a mule, with a neat pompadour on his high, intellectual forehead and a carefully shingled tail, named Chiquita, meaning, in Spanish, Little One; which was a joke, because this mule was not little. The time before when I visited the canyon I rode a mule called Martha. I rode her for three days; and never after that, they told me, was she the mule she had been. She seemed to pine away and grow morose; and every time another fat man appeared in riding togs and the guide approached her, bearing a saddle, she laid down on her side and uttered low moans. I judge she suffered from melancholia or something of that general nature; so now I had Chiquita for a mount.

We headed down the Hermit Trail. When we came to the first sign post on the journey Chiquita stopped dead still and read what it said. And when she read that we had gone only eight hundred feet below the level of the rim and had yet nearly four thousand feet to go, measuring straight downward—or nine miles as the trail ran—realization seemed to come to her, and she turned and put her head on my shoulder and sobbed out the sorrow of her heart. I joined with her; for I remember that it had been more than a year since I had ridden in a saddle, and this was a very hard saddle. And I am tender, if you get my meaning. There, on the narrow ledge overhanging the abysmal depths, our tears mingled.

Shortly afterward my attention was distracted. The scientist with the whiskers sat down in his white-duck riding pants on a cactus bed. But, before that, the young lady from Waukesha pulled her mule out of line and hurried him forward from the middle of the cavalcade to the head of it, so she might ask Shorty, who was our chief guide for that day, some questions that had been accumulating and backing up in her during the earlier stages of the expedition. She had been repeatedly assured in various quarters that she was perfectly safe, and that the trail was perfectly safe, and that everything was perfectly safe; but still she craved confirmation from an expert and experienced source.

"Now tell me honestly," she demanded: "isn't there any danger at all connected with this ride?"

"Ma'am," said Shorty seriously, "since you put it up to me that way, I ain't going to deceive you. If Slim's wife is running things down to the foot of the trail everything is all right, and you needn't worry; but if she should 'a' happened to leave camp and Slim should be doing the cooking, and we should have to eat his cooking to-night for supper, this shore is what you might call a perilous journey."

That satisfied her for a while; but presently she saw one of those little monuments of piled-up bowlders the canyon prospectors leave behind them to mark the locations of their mining claims, and she wanted to know what that was. The guides are always set and loaded for that question; they know that some time during the trip, sooner or later, it is coming, and they are primed for it.

"That, ma'am," said Shorty in an Alas-poor-Yorick-I-Knew-him-well tone, "is the grave of a poor old trail guide."

Shorty was waiting for some one of the party to ask what caused the death of the late lamented, so that he might reply, according to the ancient ritual, that he was talked to death by tourists, when the scientist made his mistake. The scientist had joined us at the last moment, wearing an outfit of gorgeous and luxuriant red whiskers, a pair of form-fitting white-duck riding breeches, and an air of deep abstraction. Why a person so concerned with the serious aspects of life elected, even for a day, to join an assorted group of more or less frivolous-minded strangers was past telling.

BEAUTY SPOTS OF THE WORLD
The Grand Canyon of the Colorado

With half an eye, one could tell that behind the crimson ramblers lurked a mind which would see in the beauties of the heavens only an opportunity to slip up behind some playful, twittering little comet that never had done him any harm and try to throw scientific salt on its tail. To him the Grand Canyon was only worth while as offering an opportunity to prowl about in it and knock little dornicks off of it with a hammer, and then to label them and classify them, and from study of them to try to find out their mother's age.

Figuring out the birthdays of a Grand Canyon may be an absorbing occupation to such as care for that sort of thing, but they do not make exciting companions. When they sit still and think, they are static, and when they talk, they are statistical.

For an hour or so he rode with us, saying never a word. Then he came to a breathing place, where the trail widened out into a little shelflike ledge hanging over a cranny a thousand feet or so deep, and he dismounted from his mule; and, the better to rest himself, he threw his person prone on the earth at a spot where intermittent desert verdure sprouted. I imagined that he specialized in astronomy and geology rather than in botany. Probably up until that time all members of the vegetable kingdom had looked alike to him.

He dropped down right where a sprout of cactus grew, which was set thick with long, prickly spines; and, as I have already told you, he was wearing snug-fitting duck pants. He rose, as you might say, practically immediately. Once in the German trenches before Rheims I was present when a shell from the French lines dropped almost between the spraddled legs of a correspondent as he sat on a pile of turf, and at the time I thought he got from there in a fairly brisk manner; but—shucks! alongside of our scientist he was practically a stationary object. It was almost like an optical delusion. * * *

Late the next day, as we were nearing the top of the canyon, we met a lone guide coming down with a burro pack train, and he stopped long enough to tell us the finish of the story concerning the iron-jawed lady who had insisted, the morning before, on walking down.

Shortly before dusk of the same day someone passing through the Indian Gardens had heard her pants for help, and he telephoned up; and a rescue expedition was organized and sent down for the lady. She made the return trip on a mule or a couple of mules—I forget which—with a guide walking at each side, holding her hands; and when she reached the rim she went to pieces like a glass snake.

Mark Twain and A. G. MacDonnell
Two Views of Christian
Charity 1872 & 1935

OUR STAY IN SALT LAKE CITY amounted to only two days, and therefore we had no time to make the customary inquisition into the workings of polygamy and get up the usual statistics and deductions preparatory to calling the attention of the nation at large once more to the matter. I had the will to do it. With the gushing self-sufficiency of youth I was feverish to plunge in headlong and achieve a great reform here—until I saw the Mormon women. Then I was touched. My heart was wiser than my head. It warmed toward these poor, ungainly, and pathetically "homely" creatures, and as I turned to hide the generous moisture in my eyes, I said, "No—the man that marries one of them has done an act of Christian charity which entitles him to the kindly applause of mankind, not their harsh censure—and the man that marries sixty of them has done a deed of open-handed generosity so sublime that the nations should stand uncovered in his presence and worship in silence."

I ENJOYED SALT LAKE CITY and its queer, earnest people. They talk a great deal, but you get the impression that they mean what they say.

And there were more pretty girls to every square yard of sidewalk in Salt Lake City than in any city I had yet visited. The town is full of them. I asked several people for the cause of this pleasing phenomenon, but each gave a different cause. One, an ardent young ex-Missioner who had recently come back from his proselytizing sojourn in foreign parts, treated it as a matter of course. The same all-protecting Deity which sent the seagulls, also sent the standard of Beauty. Another, obviously a Rationalist, put it down to the salty air from the Great Lake which, he said, produced the dazzling colouring and the lovely skins, which a third, a morose gentleman who was travelling the country in an apparently vain endeavour to sell some mechanical device for doing something or other—he explained it to me at great length in the lounge, but I did not understand a word—brightened for a moment and said, "Ah! but you should see Kentucky," and retired again behind a rampart of typescript. But whatever the cause, there is the fact. The ladies of Salt Lake City are very beautiful.

Mark Twain
Plain Deserted 1872

I T WAS EASY ENOUGH to cross a desert in the night while we were asleep; and it was pleasant to reflect, in the morning, that we in actual person *had* encountered an absolute desert and could always speak knowingly of deserts in presence of the ignorant thenceforward. And it was pleasant also to reflect that this was not an obscure, back country desert, but a very celebrated one, the metropolis itself, as you may say. All this was very well and very comfortable and satisfactory—but now we were to cross a desert in *daylight*. This was fine—novel—romantic—dramatically adventurous—*this,* indeed, was worth living for, worth traveling for! We would write home all about it.

This enthusiasm, this stern thirst for adventure, wilted under the sultry August sun and did not last above one hour. One poor little hour—and then we were ashamed that we had "gushed" so. The poetry was all in the anticipation—there is none in the reality.

Robert Jungk
Birthmark of the New Era 1954

NO ONE GOT OUT AT ALAMOGORDO. It must be the rain, I thought. It almost never rains in New Mexico, and when for once the heavens open up everybody who can stays at home. A poor day, therefore, to ask your way to an object of interest not on the map. The half-frozen Indian squaw standing in the luggage-room, blue with cold, had no idea what I was talking about, and the stationmaster was equally nonplussed. The waitress in the Café Plaza had at least heard of the "big hole". But she advised me to keep away from it. A certain Pancho Gonzales had grazed his sheep there against the regulation, had fallen asleep and a couple of weeks later had been admitted to the county hospital. "He got too much radictivity," she said as she served the scrambled eggs. An ill-shaven man at the next table looked up from his newspaper. "Radioactivity, Alice. . ." She replied, somewhat piqued, "So what?"

The man with the newspaper was right when he advised me not to visit the place without a permit from the military authorities. I realized this an hour later as I stood before a high fence and read a yellow sign. This said in red letters in English and Spanish, "Danger. No admittance." I had travelled a few thousand miles to see the crater birthmark of a new era made by the explosion of the first atom bomb. I was standing before grills and *no admittance* signs. This was the new era, all right. No mistaking it. * * *

After the long-waited "clearance" had materialized from somewhere in the bureau beyond, they gave me a soldier as a companion on my visit to the atomic crater. This healthy square-built boy simply could not understand why anyone should expend so much patience on seeing this "bit of nothing in the middle of nothing at all."

After he had led me to the barbed-wire-enclosed rim of the large, astonishingly flat sand plateau which had come into being when the first bomb was released from the thirty-seven foot high control tower on zero point of the testing-ground, he returned to his seat at the wheel of his jeep and thumbed over the coloured pages of his comics.

The crater was covered in many places by a green mineral layer like a sort of scurf, formed in the seething white fire of the explosion. They call this slime-coloured lamina "trinitite"—"trinity stone"—after the codeword "Trinity" by which the first trial, in 1945, was designated. Splinters of trinitite, sealed in transparent plastic, are secretly sold as souvenirs round about Alamogordo. My armed escort carried one of these tiny symbols of the times with him in his wallet together with the photos of parents, relatives and a variety of girl friends.

If one picks up the trinity stone it crumbles with surprising speed. This has been a help to the desert grasses, mosses, cow-parsley and other vegetation which have grown here in the wilderness since time immemorial. In the few years that have passed since the test, plants have been able to break through the glassy green layer of death in a thousand places. In another few years they will fill the entire crater.

"Drop that thing!" the Cerberus called to me. "It's still live." I obediently let drop my radioactive bit of trinitite, threw a last glance at the large ugly scar and turned to go. "Can't think why they don't simply fill the thing up," said the

G.I. "Such a nuisance." With that we started on our return journey.

Translated from the German by Marguerite Waldman

Rudyard Kipling
A Wicked Waste 1889

ONCE UPON A TIME there was a carter who brought his team and a friend into the Yellowstone Park without due thought. Presently they came upon a few of the natural beauties of the place, and that carter turned his team into his friend's team howling: "Get back o' this, Jim. All Hell's alight under our noses." And they call the place Hell's Half-acre to this day. We, too, the old lady from Chicago, her husband, Tom, and the good little mares came to Hell's Half-acre, which is about sixty acres, and when Tom said: "Would you like to drive over it?" we said: "Certainly no, and if you do, we shall report you to the authorities." There was a plain, blistered and peeled and abominable, and it was given over to the sportings and spoutings of devils who threw mud and steam and dirt at each other with whoops and halloos and bellowing curses. The place smelt of the refuse of the Pit, and that odor mixed with the clean, wholesome aroma of the pines in our nostrils throughout the day. * * *

Imagine mighty green fields splattered with lime beds: all the flowers of the summer growing up to the very edge of the lime. That was the first glimpse of the geyser basins. The buggy had pulled up close to a rough, broken, blistered cone of stuff between ten and twenty feet high. There was trouble in that place—moaning, splashing, gurgling and the clank of machinery. A spurt of boiling water jumped into the air and a wash of water followed. I removed swiftly. The old lady from Chicago shrieked. "What a wicked waste!" said her husband. I think they call it the Riverside Geyser. Its spout was torn and ragged like the mouth of a gun when a shell has burst there. It grumbled madly for a moment or two and then was still. I crept over the steaming lime—it was the burning marl on which Satan lay—and looked fearfully down its mouth. You should never look a gift geyser in the mouth. I beheld a horrible slippery slimy funnel with water rising and falling ten feet at a time. Then the water rose to lip level with a rush and an infernal bubbling troubled this Devil's Bethesda before the sullen heave of the crest of a wave lapped over the edge and made me run. Mark the nature of the human soul! I had begun with awe, not to say terror. I stepped back from the flanks of the Riverside Geyser saying: "Pooh! Is that all it can do?" Yet for aught I knew the whole thing might have blown up at a minute's notice; she, he, or it being an arrangement of uncertain temper. * * *

The old lady from Chicago poked with her parasol at the pools as though they had been alive. On one particularly innocent-looking little puddle she turned her back for a moment, and there rose behind her a twenty-foot column of water and steam. Then she shrieked and protested that "she never thought it would ha' done it," and the old man chewed his tobacco steadily, and mourned for steam power wasted. I embraced the whitened stump of a middle-sized pine that had grown all too close to a hot pool's lip, and the whole thing turned over under my hand as a tree would do in a nightmare. * * *

We rounded a low spur of hill, and came out upon a field of aching snowy lime, rolled in sheets, twisted into knots, riven with rents and diamonds and stars, stretching for more than half a mile in every direction. In this place of despair lay most of the big geysers who know when there is trouble in Krakatoa, who tell the pines when there is a cyclone on the Atlantic seaboard, and who—are exhibited to visitors under pretty and fanciful names. The first mound that I encountered belonged to a goblin splashing in his tub. I heard him kick, pull a showerbath on his shoulders, gasp, crack his joints, and rub himself down with a towel; then he let the water out of the bath, as a thoughtful man should, and it all sank down out of sight till another goblin arrived. Yet they called this place the Lioness and the Cubs. * * *

Would you believe that even these terrible creatures have to be guarded by the troopers to prevent the irreverent American from chipping the cones to pieces, or worse still, making the geysers sick? If you take of soft-soap a small barrelful and drop it down a geyser's mouth, the geyser will presently be forced to lay all before you and for days afterwards will be of an irritated and inconsistent stomach. Now I wish that I had stolen soap and tried the experiment on some lonely little beast of a geyser in the woods. It sounds so probable—and so human. * * *

We went over to Old Faithful, who by reason of his faithfulness has benches close to him whence you may comfortably watch. At the appointed hour we heard the water flying up and down the mouth with the sob of waves in a cave. Then came the preliminary gouts, then a roar and a rush, and that glittering column of diamonds rose, quivered, stood still for a minute. Then it broke, and the rest was a confused snarl of water not thirty feet high. All the young ladies—not more than twenty—in the tourist band remarked that it was "elegant," and betook themselves to writing their names in the bottoms of shallow pools. Nature fixes the insult indelibly, and the after-years will learn that "Hattie," "Sadie," "Mamie," "Sophie," and so forth, have taken out their hairpins, and scrawled in the face of Old Faithful.

Wholehearted joy is what everyone hopes for when on vacation, but experiences too rarely, at least as an adult. Let's share Rudyard Kipling's joy as he fishes for salmon in Oregon.

Rudyard Kipling
The Best That It Yields 1889

I HAVE LIVED! The American Continent may now sink
under the sea, for I have taken the best that it yields, and
the best was neither dollars, love, nor real estate.

Hear now, gentlemen of the Punjab Fishing Club, who
whip the reaches of the Tavi, and you who painfully import
trout to Ootacamund, and I will tell you how "old man
California" and I went fishing, and you shall envy. * * *

We reached Portland, California and I, crying for salmon,
and the real-estate man, to whom we had been intrusted by
"Portland" the insurance man, met us in the street saying
that fifteen miles away, across country, we should come
upon a place called Clackamas where we might perchance
find what we desired. And California, his coat-tails flying in
the wind, ran to a livery stable and chartered a wagon and
team forthwith. I could push the wagon about with one
hand, so light was its structure. The team was purely
American—that is to say, almost human in its intelligence
and docility. Some one said that the roads were not good on
the way to Clackamas and warned us against smashing the
springs. "Portland," who had watched the preparations,
finally reckoned "he'd come along too," and under heavenly
skies we three companions of a day set forth; California
carefully lashing our rods into the carriage, and the bystand-
ers overwhelming us with directions as to the sawmills we
were to pass, the ferries we were to cross, and the sign-posts
we were to seek signs from. * * *

Once we found a wayside camp of horsedealers lounging
by a pool, ready for a sale or a swap, and once two sun-
tanned youngsters shot down a hill on Indian ponies, their
full creels banging from the high-pommeled saddles. They
had been fishing, and were our brethren therefore. We
shouted aloud in chorus to scare a wild-cat; we squabbled

over the reasons that had led a snake to cross a road; we heaved bits of bark at a venturesome chipmunk, who was really the little gray squirrel of India and had come to call on me; we lost our way and got the wagon so beautifully fixed on a steep road that we had to tie the two hind-wheels to get it down. Above all, California told tales of Nevada and Arizona, of lonely nights spent out prospecting, of the slaughter of deer and the chase of men; of woman, lovely woman, who is a firebrand in a Western city, and leads to the popping of pistols, and of the sudden changes and chances of Fortune, who delights in making the miner or the lumberman a quadruplicate millionaire, and in "busting" the railroad king. That was a day to be remembered and it had only begun when we drew rein at a tiny farmhouse on the banks of the Clackamas and sought horse-feed and lodging ere we hastened to the river that broke over a weir not a quarter of a mile away.

Imagine a stream seventy yards broad divided by a pebbly island, running over seductive riffles, and swirling into deep, quiet pools where the good salmon goes to smoke his pipe after meals. Set such a stream and fields of breast-high crops surrounded by hills of pine, throw in where you please quiet water, log-fenced meadows, and a hundred-foot bluff just to keep the scenery from growing too monotonous, and you will get some faint notion of the Clackamas.

Portland had no rod. He held the gaff and the whisky. California sniffed, upstream and downstream across the racing water, chose his ground, and let the gaudy spoon drop in the tail of a riffle. I was getting my rod together when I heard the joyous shriek of the reel and the yells of California, and three feet of living silver leaped into the air far across the water. The forces were engaged. The salmon tore up stream, the tense line cutting the water like a tide-rip behind him, and the light bamboo bowed to breaking. What happened after I cannot tell. California swore and prayed, and Portland shouted advice, and I did all three for what appeared to be half a day, but was in reality a little over a quarter of an hour, and sullenly our fish came home with spurts of temper, dashes head-on, and sarabands in the air; but home to the bank came he, and the remorseless reel gathered up the thread of his life inch by inch. We landed him in a little bay, and the spring-weight checked at eleven and a half pounds. Eleven and one-half pounds of fighting salmon! We danced a war-dance on the pebbles, and California caught me round the waist in a hug that went near to breaking my ribs while he shouted: "Partner! Partner! This is glory! Now you catch your fish! Twenty-four years I've waited for this!"

I went into that icy-cold river and made my cast just above a weir, and all but foul-hooked a blue and black water-snake with a coral mouth who coiled herself on a stone and hissed maledictions. The next cast—ah, the pride of it, the regal splendor of it! the thrill that ran down from finger-tip to toe! The water boiled. He broke for the fly and got it! There remained enough sense in me to give him all he wanted when he jumped not once but twenty times before the upstream flight that ran my line out to the last half-dozen turns, and I saw the nickled reel-bar glitter under the thinning green coils. My thumb was burned deep when I strove to stopper the line, but I did not feel it till later, for my soul was out in the dancing water praying for him to turn ere he took my tackle away. The prayer was heard. As I bowed back, the butt of the rod on my left hip-bone and the top joint dipping like unto a weeping willow, he turned, and I accepted each inch of slack that I could by any means get in as a favor from on High. There be several sorts of success in this world that taste well in the moment of enjoyment, but I question whether the stealthy theft of line from an able-bodied salmon who knows exactly what you are doing and why you are doing it is not sweeter than any other victory within human scope. Like California's fish, he ran at me head-on and leaped against the line, but the Lord gave me two hundred and fifty pairs of fingers in that hour.

The banks and the pine trees danced dizzily round me, but I only reeled—reeled as for life—reeled for hours, and at the end of the reeling continued to give him the butt while he sulked in a pool. California was farther up the reach, and with the corner of my eye I could see him casting with long casts and much skill. Then he struck, and my fish broke for the weir at the same instant, and down the reach we came, California and I; reel answering reel, even as the morning stars sung together.

The first wild enthusiasm of capture had died away. We were both at work now in deadly earnest to prevent the lines fouling, to stall off a downstream rush for deep water just above the weir, and at the same time to get the fish into the shallow bay downstream that gave the best practicable landing. Portland bade us both be of good heart, and volunteered to take the rod from my hands. I would rather have died among the pebbles than surrender my right to play and land my first salmon, weight unknown, on an eight-ounce rod. I heard California, at my ear it seemed, gasping: "He's a fighter from Fightersville, sure!" as his fish made a fresh break across the stream. I saw Portland fall off a log fence, break the overhanging bank, and clatter down to the pebbles, all sand and landing-net, and I dropped on a log to rest for a moment. As I drew breath the weary hands slackened their hold, and I forgot to give him the butt. A wild scutter in the water, a plunge and a break for the headwaters of the Clackamas was my reward, and the hot toil of reeling-in with one eye under the water and the other on the top joint of the rod, was renewed. Worst of all, I was blocking California's path to the little landing-bay aforesaid, and he had to halt and tire his prize where he was. "The Father of all Salmon!" he shouted. "For the love of Heaven, get your *trout* to bank, Johnny Bull." But I could no more. Even the insult failed to move me. The rest of the game was with the salmon. He suffered himself to be drawn, skipping with pretended delight at getting to the haven where I would fain have him. Yet no sooner did he feel shoal water under his ponderous belly than he backed like a torpedo-boat, and the snarl of the reel told me that my labor was in vain. A dozen times at least this happened ere the line hinted he had given up that battle and would be towed in. He was towed. The landing-net was useless for one of his size, and I would not have him gaffed. I stepped into the shallows and heaved him out with a respectful hand under the gill, for which kindness he battered me about the legs with his tail, and I felt the strength of him and was proud. California had taken my place in the shallows, his fish hard held. I was up the bank lying full length on the sweet-scented grass, and gasping in company with my first salmon caught, played and landed on an eight-ounce rod. My hands were cut and bleeding. I was dripping with sweat, spangled like harlequin with scales, wet from the waist down, nose peeled by the sun, but utterly, supremely, and consummately happy. He, the beauty, the darling, the daisy, my Salmon Bahadur, weighed twelve pounds, and I had been seven and thirty minutes bringing him to bank! He had been lightly hooked on the angle of the right jaw, and the hook had not wearied him. That hour I sat among princes and crowned heads—greater than them all.

Few tourists go to California to experience an earthquake, but almost every one imagines what it would be like if. . . Well, Mark Twain, of course, happened to be in San Francisco for a biggie and, needless to say, he managed to find some humor in it. And then Czech-Canadian novelist Josef Skvorecky visits one of the strangest sights in Northern California, which means anywhere.

Mark Twain
My First Earthquake 1872

THE "CURIOSITIES" OF THE EARTHQUAKE were simply endless. Gentlemen and ladies who were sick, or were taking a siesta, or had dissipated till a late hour and were making up lost sleep thronged into the public streets in all sorts of queer apparel, and some without any at all. One woman who had been washing a naked child, ran down the street holding it by the ankles as if it were a dressed turkey. Prominent citizens who were supposed to keep the Sabbath strictly, rushed out of saloons in their shirt-sleeves, with billiard cues in their hands. Dozens of men with necks swathed in napkins, rushed from barber-shops, lathered to the eyes or with one cheek clean shaved and the other still bearing a hairy stubble. Horses broke from stables, and a frightened dog rushed up a short attic ladder and out on to a roof, and when his scare was over had not the nerve to go down again the same way he had gone up. A prominent editor flew down stairs, in the principal hotel, with nothing on but one brief undergarment—met a chambermaid, and exclaimed: "Oh, what *shall* I do! Where shall I go!"

She responded with naive serenity: "If you have no choice, you might try a clothing-store."

A certain foreign consul's lady was the acknowledged leader of fashion, and every time she appeared in anything new or extraordinary, the ladies in the vicinity made a raid on their husbands' purses and arrayed themselves similarly. One man who had suffered considerably and growled accordingly, was standing at the window when the shocks came, and the next instant the consul's wife, just out of the bath, fled by with no other apology for clothing than—a bath-towel! The sufferer rose superior to the terrors of the earthquake, and said to his wife: "Now *that* is something *like!* Get out your towel my dear!"

Josef Skvorecky
The Largest Oddest Building 1969

THIS ENORMOUS COUNTRY has hardly any history: that is, in comparison with the architectural museum of palaces and cathedrals in Mediterranean Europe, and as long as by history we mean merely the history of the most problematical mammal. But because it has, at the same time, the most passionate antiquarians, Americans restore, catalog, and classify everything that has to do with the nineteenth century. Each town has its pseudo-bronze plaque decked out with the words "Oldest House" and the fastidiously transcribed genealogy of the person who built, bought, stole, or embezzled it (here its significance ends). Each town has its stone on the spot where trappers drew up an agreement with the Indians (later repudiated). Instead of Gothic and Renaissance ceremonial buildings, there are architectural curiosities inspired not by the Romans, but by fairy tales and phantasmagorias. * * *

Go south from the city of Santa Rosa, bypass Frisco and its bridges of pearl, which from afar resemble drinking brontosauruses, and you will find yourself approaching the city of Santa Clara. Everywhere along the road you find signs enticing you to visit the **WINCHESTER MYSTERY HOUSE, THE LARGEST ODDEST BUILDING IN THE WORLD.** The contiguity of superlatives unseparated by a comma is illogical, but American; certainly the Winchester House cannot take upon itself the right to surpass the proportions of, say, the Doges' Palace, but because America is traditionally the land of everything that is *most,* the ordinary superlative does not eliminate all other members of the category. Next to the merely "odd" houses there are the "oddest" houses, and of these the Winchester happens to be the largest.

Sarah L. Winchester was the widow of the owner of the

factory that made the celebrated Winchester, the weapon of the riflemen and the buffalo hunters, whom you meet in each of Zane Grey's novels. The business was lucrative, even after the industrialist's death. It is said that day after day a clear profit of a thousand dollars, and possibly more, dropped into the widow's piggy-bank. And the thirty-six-year-old widow turned that everlasting source of gold into a wooden monstrosity.

Why? The death of her husband, who was followed to the grave by their daughter, destroyed the odd woman's optimistic American world. She tried to counteract the cruelty of death in a typically American way: spiritualism. And so she built a residence where she could converse with spirits, and some sort of fortune-teller—whose motives, if we appreciate the wealth of her client, were understandable—convinced her that she and no other, Mrs. Sarah L. Winchester, was predestined to immortality. Under one condition, of course: she would live only as long as she did not stop building her house.

So a group of masons, carpenters, glaziers, and plumbers had an excellent job for thirty-six years. Then, at the age of eighty-five, despite the prophecy, Mrs. Sarah died, and the golden age of the artisans came to an end. Relatives weren't very keen on living in the house; instead they rented a truck and spent an entire year plundering the luxurious fixtures inside. Thereafter, the house remained bare and empty; once in the fashionable style of American Art Nouveau, now suggested only by a few splendid Tiffany stained-glass windows bent by an earthquake. Otherwise there is only dust, cobwebs, and joke-cracking tourists.

It was built for the summoning as well as the beguiling of spirits. It rises up without symmetry and without system, like a mammoth child's fold-up toy, covering six acres and containing 160 rooms. Its architectural principles consist of mystical numbers: rooms have thirteen windows; forty flights of stairs have thirteen steps each (in order for there to be thirteen, several of the steps were built for dwarves);

the chandeliers spread out thirteen bony arms, and the ceilings are composed of thirteen panels. Somewhere near the middle of the house, as if in the mother-cell of an anthill, there is a closet. Open it and you'll discover that through the closet it is possible to enter a room without any doors or windows, in which Madame communicated with the good spirits of her daughter and her husband. Evil spirits were not supposed to enter this room, so the handy carpenters did everything they could to keep the spirits from getting into Mrs. Winchester's private boudoir. A good half of the forty staircases lead nowhere: after much winding they end in a wall. You enter through enormous carved doors—as a matter of fact, you don't enter: you look into a little room where dolls might dine, but, on the contrary, the dining room is reached by squeezing through a drawer. Elsewhere, a corridor goes topsy-turvy: all at once you have the impression that you're changing into a fly, because you are walking along the paneled ceiling and upside-down candlesticks jut out of the ceiling-ground as high as your waist; Corinthian columns stand upside down, and you crawl along the tops of doorframes, a good meter above the panels below you. Everything was done to give the spirits schizophrenia. * * *

A small group of tourists, whom I'd dragged here from the site of a gaudily-colored festival in the town of St. Joseph, were disgruntled. They nearly bawled me out. There is nothing here. Crap: they looked around the bare, worm-eaten walls, which had not been sanctified by the touch of the hands of famous artists out of textbooks and which could certainly not be compared with the Sistine Chapel. Only I don't trust them. A woman explained how, in the famous chapel, she had sat the whole day through and stared in ecstasy at Michelangelo's frescoes on the ceiling. I sat there too. In order for someone to delight in those frescoes, he has to be unusually farsighted or he must look at them through binoculars. They're too high.

I don't know: can marble statues in a Florentine square move people who are not at all touched by the freakish wooden mausoleum of a human tragedy that is certainly not one of the greatest, but human nevertheless? Maybe I'm defective. Saint Peter's, which was designed for the subjective diminution of man, does not inspire me to meditation nearly so much as the tiny Romanesque church in Trebonic, near Prague; possibly because there, evidently, they believed in something, whereas here I cannot shake the impression that most people pretend, and a concept attired in ermine becomes, oddly, flat. The paintings of da Vinci in the Doges' Palace were not as close to my heart as the primitive paintings in the rooms at Pompeii, whose immortality is due not to their genius, but to natural catastrophe.

I don't know. In the end, considering how disgruntled the tourists were when wanting to look at majorettes they found a heap of old wood, I imagined something having to do with the rear end of a body and headed for Disneyland.

Translated from the Czech by the editor

CALIFORNIA

Arnold Roth. By permission of Punch Publications Ltd.

Los Angeles is almost as controversial a city as New York. Hollywood, pollution, beaches, Watts: it's got everything America has, and if anything's missing, it can be constructed on the lot.

But for tourists, domestic and foreign, Los Angeles is closer to its name than its reputation: the city where dreams come true in video form. Classic American humorist S. J. Perelman descends upon Hollywood with his trigger finger on all the clichés. And then Leopold Tyrmand shares an anecdote which shows that even in Los Angeles there are limits, if not city ones.

S. J. Perelman
Strictly From Hunger 1944

THE VIOLET HUSH OF TWILIGHT was descending over Los Angeles as my hostess, Violet Hush, and I left its suburbs headed toward Hollywood. In the distance a glow of huge piles of burning motion-picture scripts lit up the sky. The crisp tang of frying writers and directors whetted my appetite. How good it was to be alive, I thought, inhaling deep lungfuls of carbon monoxide. Suddenly our powerful Gatti-Cazazza slid to a stop in the traffic.

"What is it, Jenkin?" Violet called anxiously through the speaking-tube to the chauffeur (played by Lyle Talbot).

A *suttee* was in progress by the roadside, he said—did we wish to see it? Quickly Violet and I elbowed our way through the crowd. An enormous funeral pyre composed of thousands of feet of film and scripts, drenched with Chanel Number Five, awaited the torch of Jack Holt, who was to act as master of ceremonies. In a few terse words Violet explained this unusual custom borrowed from the Hindus and never paid for. The worst disgrace that can befall a producer is an unkind notice from a New York reviewer. When this happens, the producer becomes a pariah in Hollywood. He is shunned by his friends, thrown into bankruptcy, and like a Japanese electing hara-kiri, he commits *suttee*. A great bonfire is made of the film, and the luckless producer, followed by directors, actors, technicians, and the producer's wives, immolate themselves. Only the scenario writers are exempt. These are tied between the tails of two spirited Caucasian ponies, which are then driven off in opposite directions. This custom is called "a conference."

Violet and I watched the scene breathlessly. Near us Harry Cohn, head of Columbia Studios, was being rubbed with huck towels preparatory to throwing himself into the flames. He was nonchalantly smoking a Rocky Ford five-center, and the man's courage drew a tear to the eye of even the most callous. Weeping relatives besought him to eschew his design, but he stood adamant. Adamant Eve, his plucky secretary, was being rubbed with crash towels preparatory to flinging herself into Cohn's embers. Assistant directors busily prepared spears, war-bonnets and bags of pemmican which the Great Chief would need on his trip to the "Happy Hunting Grounds." Wampas and beads to placate the Great Spirit (played by Will Hays) were piled high about the stoical tribesman.

Suddenly Jack Holt (played by Edmund Lowe) raised his hand for silence. The moment had come. With bowed head Holt made a simple invocation couched in one-syllable words so that even the executives might understand. Throwing his five-center to a group of autograph-hunters, the great man poised himself for the fatal leap. * * *

When Violet and I finally stole away to our waiting motor, we felt that we were somehow nearer to each other. I snuggled luxuriously into the buffalo lap-robe Violet had provided against the treacherous night air and gazed out at the gleaming neon lights. Soon we would be in Beverly Hills, and already the quaint native women were swarming alongside in their punts urging us to buy their cunning beadwork and mangoes. . . . It seemed but a moment before we were sliding under the portecochère of her home, a magnificent rambling structure of beaverboard patterned after an Italian ropewalk of the sixteenth century. It had recently been remodeled by a family of wrens who had introduced chewing-gum into the left wing, and only three or four obscure Saxon words could do it justice. * * *

After a copious dinner, melting-eyed beauties in lacy black underthings fought with each other to serve me kummel. A hurried apology, and I was curled up in bed with the Autumn, 1927, issue of *The Yale Review*. Halfway through an exciting symposium on Sir Thomas Aquinas' indebtedness to Professors Whitehead and Spengler, I suddenly detected a stowaway blonde under the bed. Turning a deaf ear to her heartrending entreaties and burning glances, I sent her packing. Then I treated my face to a feast of skin food, buried my head in the pillow and went bye-bye.

Hollywood Boulevard! I rolled the rich syllables over on my tongue and thirstily drank in the beauty of the scene before me. On all sides nattily attired boulevardiers clad in rich stuffs strolled nonchalantly, inhaling cubebs and exchanging epigrams stolen from Martial and Wilde. Thousands of scantily draped but none the less appetizing extra girls milled past me, their mouths a scarlet wound and their eyes clearly defined in their faces. Their voluptuous curves set my blood on fire, and as I made my way down Mammary Lane, a strange thought began to invade my brain: I realized that I had not eaten breakfast yet. In a Chinese eatery cunningly built in the shape of an old shoe I managed to assuage the inner man with a chopped glove salad topped off with frosted cocoa. Charming platinum-haired hostesses in red pajamas and peaked caps added a note of color to the surroundings, whilst a gypsy orchestra played selections from Victor Herbert's operettas on musical saws. It was a bit of old Vienna come to life, and the sun was a red ball in the heavens before I realized with a start that I had promised to report at the Plushnick Studios.

Commandeering a taxicab, I arrived at the studio just in time to witness the impressive ceremony of changing the guard. In the central parade ground, on a snowy white charger, sat Max Plushnick, resplendent in a producer's uniform, his chest glittering with first mortgage liens, amortizations, and estoppels. His personal guard, composed of picked vice-presidents of the Chase National Bank, was drawn up stiffly about him in a hollow square.

But the occasion was not a happy one. A writer had been caught trying to create an adult picture. The drums rolled dismally, and the writer, his head sunk on his chest, was led out amid a ghastly silence. With the aid of a small stepladder Plushnick slid lightly from his steed. Sternly he ripped the epaulets and buttons from the traitor's tunic, broke his sword across his knee, and in a few harsh words demoted him to the mail department.

"And now," began Plushnick, "I further condemn you to eat. . ."

"No, no!" screamed the poor wretch, falling to his knees and embracing Plushnick's jack boots, "not that, not that!"

"Stand up, man," ordered Plushnick, his lip curling. "I condemn you to eat in the studio restaurant for ten days and may God have mercy on your soul." The awful words rang out on the still evening air and even Plushnick's hardened old mercenaries shuddered. The heartrending cries of the unfortunate were drowned in the boom of the sunset gun.

In the wardrobe department I was photographed, fingerprinted, and measured for the smock and Windsor tie which was to be my uniform. A nameless fear clutched at my heart as two impassive turnkeys herded me down a corridor to my supervisor's office. For what seemed hours we waited in an anteroom. Then my serial number was called, the legirons were struck off, and I was shoved through a door into the presence of Diana ffrench-Mamoulian.

How to describe what followed? Diana ffrench-Mamoulian was accustomed to having her way with writers, and my long lashes and peachblow mouth seemed to whip her to insensate desire. In vain, time and again, I tried to bring her attention back to the story we were discussing, only to find her gem-incrusted fingers straying through my hair. When our interview was over, her cynical attempt to "date me up" made every fiber of my being cry out in revolt.

"P-please," I stammered, my face burning, "I—I wish you wouldn't. . . . I'm engaged to a Tri Kappa at Goucher—"

"Just one kiss," she pleaded, her breath hot against my neck. In desperation I granted her boon, knowing full well that my weak defences were crumbling before the onslaught of this love tigree. Finally she allowed me to leave, but only after I had promised to dine at her penthouse apartment and have an intimate chat about the script. The basket of slave bracelets and marzipan I found awaiting me on my return home made me realize to what lengths Diana would go.

I was radiant that night in blue velvet tails and a boutonnière of diamonds from Cartier's, my eyes starry and the merest hint of cologne at my ear-lobes. An inscrutable Oriental served the Lucullan repast and my vis-à-vis was as effervescent as the wine.

"Have a bit of the wine, darling?" queried Diana solicitously, indicating the roast Long Island airplane with applesauce. I tried to turn our conversation from the personal note, but Diana would have none of it. Soon we were exchanging gay bantam over the mellow Vouvray, laughing as we dipped fastidious fingers into the Crisco parfait for which Diana was famous. Our meal finished, we sauntered into the rumpus room and Diana turned on the radio. With a savage snarl the radio turned on her and we slid over the waxed floor in the intricate maze of the jackdaw strut. Without quite knowing why, I found myself hesitating before the plate of liqueur candies Diana was pressing on me.

"I don't think I should—really, I'm a trifle faint—"

"Oh, come on," she urged masterfully. "After all, you're old enough to be your father—I mean I'm old enough to be my mother. . . ." She stuffed a brandy bonbon between my clenched teeth. Before long I was eating them thirstily, reeling about the room and shouting snatches of coarse drunken doggerel. My brain was on fire, I tell you. Through the haze I saw Diana ffrench-Mamoulian, her nostrils dilated, groping for me. My scream of terror only egged her on, overturning chairs and tables in her bestial pursuit. With superhuman talons she tore off my collar and suspenders. I sank to my knees, choked with sobs, hanging on to my last shirt-stud like a drowning man. Her Svengali eyes were slowly hypnotizing me; I fought like a wounded bird—and then, blissful unconsciousness.

When I came to, the Oriental servant and Diana were battling in the center of the floor. As I watched, Yen Shee Gow drove a well-aimed blow to her mid-section, following it with a right cross to the jaw. Diana staggered and rolled under a table. Before my astonished eyes John Chinaman stripped the mask from his face and revealed the features of Blanche Almonds, a little seamstress I had long wooed unsuccessfully in New York. Gently she bathed my temples with Florida water and explained how she had followed me, suspecting Diana ffrench-Mamoulian's intentions. I let her rain kisses over my face and lay back in her arms as beaming Ivan tucked us in and cracked his whip over the prancing bays. In a few seconds our sleigh was skimming over the hard crust toward Port Arthur and freedom, leaving Plushnick's discomfited officers gnashing one another's teeth. The wintry Siberian moon glowed over the tundras, drenching my hair with moonbeams for Blanche to kiss away. And so, across the silvery steppes amid the howling of wolves, we rode into a new destiny, purified in the crucible that men call Hollywood.

Leopold Tyrmand
Neverending L.A. 1970

IN ONE OF EMILE ZOLA'S NOVELS, the hero stands at the window of a train approaching Paris; the hero contemplates the roofs of the capital and vows to master the city, to conquer it. He was fortunate not to come to Los Angeles. How is it possible to conquer a city where even decent sight-seeing is impossible? Just leaving my hotel I feel lost—the distance to the nearest drugstore is the same as between two villages in France. One's helplessness in such vastness is paralyzing. In a car with an attractive girl, I said: "Let's go somewhere out of town. . .," having in mind eventual kissing. "But where?" she asked. "Oh, no matter where. . .," I smiled, trying to hide my intentions, ". . .where the city ends." "Los Angeles never ends," she said firmly.

Hawaii. Land of beaches, palms, pineapples, and the hula. A lot of fun can be made about the parking lot much of this paradise has become, but British writer Somerset Maugham looks at something far from paradise—a volcano—and shares with us the opposing views of two tourists.

Somerset Maugham
God or Hell? 1949

KILAUEA. The volcano is on Hawaii, the largest island of the group. You land at Hilo and drive up, first through fields of rice and sugar-cane and then, climbing all the time, through a forest of great tree-ferns. They are weird and strange like the imaginations of some draughtsman of the horrible. All manner of climbing plants wind around the trees in an impenetrable tangle. Gradually the vegetation stops and you come to the lava field, grey, dead, silent; here no plants grow and no birds sing; you see the smoke rising, here and there thickly, in other places ascending thin and straight like the smoke from a cottage chimney. You get out and walk. The lava crunches under your feet. Now and then you step over narrow fissures from which the sulphurous smoke rises, making you cough. You come to the jagged edge of the crater. Nothing has prepared you for the sight. It is stupendous and alarming. You look down upon a vast sea of lava. It is black and heavy. It is in perpetual movement. The lava is only a thin crust and it is broken at irregular intervals by gashes of red fire, and here and there again are geysers of flame rising into the air, thirty, or forty, or fifty feet. They spurt up, white hot, like artificial fountains. The two most impressive things are the roar: it is like the roar of surf on a gloomy day, as unceasing, or like the roar of a cataract, as formidable; and secondly the movement: the lava moves on, on, all the time, with a stealthy movement in which you may almost see the purpose of a living thing. There is something strangely determined about its quiet progress, it has a malign tenacity; and yet it transcends anything living, it has the inevitableness of fate and the ruthlessness of time. The lava is like some huge formless creature born of primeval slime crawling slowly in pursuit of some loathsome prey. The lava moves forward steadily towards a fiery gap and then seems to fall into a bottomless cavern of flame. You see vast holes of fire, great caves of flame. A man standing near said: "Gosh, it's like hell," but a priest beside him turned and said: "No, it is like the face of God."

≈Return

≈The last thing we think about when we plan our vacations and anticipate the fun we'll have, the places we'll see, and the things we'll do, is what we'll bring home for our family and friends. We know we have to; we know we'll spend a good portion of our time (especially the time we allot to arguments) agonizing about what's right for Aunt Agnes or, if we put it all off until we get to the airport for the return flight, agonizing about whether Aunt Agnes will notice that her gift was bought at an airport. To put the last touches on this guidebook, here's Phyllis McGinley, the only light-versist to win a Pulitzer Prize, waxing poetic on the prosaic subject of souvenirs.

Phyllis McGinley
A Dream of Gifties 1961

Somewhere somebody sits
   (In a cave, in a cell, in a tower)—
Somebody out of his wits
   But primed with lunatic power.
And what is he doing when midnight's brewing
   And mocking moons sail high?
Inventing with sneers the Souvenirs
   That summer tourists buy;
With sneers and jeers and lunatic leers
Inventing the roadside Souvenirs
   That motoring tourists buy:

Balsam pillows in dubious felts,
Handpainted neckties,
Wampum belts,
Perfumes harsher
Than laws by Dracon,
Plates with pictures of Echo Lake on,
Pottery gnomes for cluttering yards
And plaid, unplayable playing-cards.

No Gift Shop stands so bleak,
    Motel so poor but has'm,
From Pike's memorial peak
    To dark Ausable Chasm.
At soda fountains in the Rocky Mountains,
    At southern inns gardenious,
Behold rich rows of the curios
    Spawned by his nightmare genius:

Pots of cactuses, gray and scratchy,
Moccasins spurned
By the poorest Apache,
Incense burners
Like skulls and hearses,
Raffia baskets, raffia purses,
Leather-work calendars slightly singed,
And all designed by a mind unhinged.

They lurk with a smirk obscene
    In a thousand Parks and Grottos
Where all of the soap is green
    And all of the mugs wear mottos.
From seashore tavern to Carlsbad Cavern,
    Wherever the Buicks roam,
You can trace his tracks by the pennants and plaques
    That motorists carry home,
The terrible stacks of pennants and plaques
That ladies in slacks with sunburnt backs
    Bemusedly carry home,

While he laughs Ha Ha and he snorts Hey Hey.
Oh, I had a horrible
Thought today!
When soon our astronauts
Raid the stars,
What will they fetch from the fields of Mars?
Souvenir spoons in a matching set
And a pink Saint Christopher statuette.

The tour's over. All bets are off. It's curtains for this book. I hope that traveling through America will never be quite the same for you. That the sameness of hotels will seem more ridiculous than boring; that you will start having conversations with road signs and the long-gone occupants of the sights you visit; that the people you meet (and are) will appear more interesting or, at least, more comical and . . . well . . . human. In short, I wish you a topsy-turvy vacation or two through the wilds and calms of the United States. Enjoy!

Acknowledgments

ALEX ATKINSON: Excerpts from *By Rocking-Chair Across America* by Alex Atkinson and Ronald Searle. Copyright © 1959 by Funk & Wagnalls, Co. Reprinted by permission of HarperCollins Publishers. RUSSELL BAKER: Copyright © 1979 by The New York Times Company. Reprinted by permission. SIMONE DE BEAUVOIR: From *America Day by Day* by Simone de Beauvoir, translated by Patrick Dudley. Copyright 1953 by Grove Press. Used by permission of Grove Press, Inc. LUDWIG BEMELMANS: Reprinted by permission of International Creative Management, Inc. Copyright © 1942 by Ludwig Bemelmans, Viking. ROBERT BENCHLEY: "The Homelike Hotel" from *Benchley Beside Himself* by Robert Benchley. Copyright 1930 by Robert Benchley, 1943 by Harper & Row, Publishers, Inc. Reprinted by permission of HarperCollins Publishers. BILL BRYSON: Excerpts from *The Lost Continent* by Bill Bryson. Copyright © by Bill Bryson. Reprinted by permission of HarperCollins Publishers and Martin Secker & Warburg Ltd. ART BUCHWALD: Reprinted from *While Reagan Slept,* Putnam, 1983, by permission of the author. ROBERTSON DAVIES: From *The Papers of Samuel Marchbanks* by Robertson Davies. Copyright © 1986 by Robertson Davies. Reprinted by permission of Viking Penguin, a division of Penguin Books USA Inc., and Stoddart Publishing Co., Ltd. E. M. DELAFIELD: Reprinted from *The Provincial Lady in America* by E. M. Delafield, © 1934 E. M. Delafield, by permission of Macmillan London Ltd. ALLEN DRURY: Reprinted from *Advise & Consent* by Allen Drury, © 1959 Allen Drury, by permission of the Robert Lantz-Joy Harris Literary Agency. H. F. ELLIS: Reprinted by permission. Copyright © 1960, 1987 The New Yorker Magazine, Inc. IAN FRAZIER: "Into the American Maw" from *Dating Your Mom* by Ian Frazier. Copyright © 1980, 1986 Ian Frazier. Reprinted by permission of Farrar, Straus & Giroux, Inc. WILLIAM GOLDING: Reprinted from *The Hot Gates and Other Occasional Pieces* by William Golding, © 1965 William Golding, by permission of Faber & Faber Ltd. BOB GREENE: Reprinted with permission of Atheneum Publishers, an imprint of Macmil-

THE HUMORISTS' GUIDES

THE HUMORISTS' GUIDES are available in better bookstores everywhere. Or, order directly by mail. Send a check or money order for $10.95 per book, plus $2.00 for shipping, no matter how many books you order (U.S. only; NJ residents, please add sales tax of 7% (77¢ per book)).

If you would like to receive information about future Catbird books on travel and humor, please send us your name and address on this form or any other way you choose. Please send orders and names to: *Catbird Press, 44 North Sixth Avenue, Highland Park, NJ 08904.* For further information, call 908-572-0816.

No. of
<u>copies</u>

> *Savoir Rire: The Humorists' Guide to France*
> *When in Rome: The Humorists' Guide to Italy*
> *In a Fog: The Humorists' Guide to England*
> *Here We Are: The Humorists' Guide to the United States*
> *All in the Same Boat: The Humorists' Guide*
> *to the Ocean Cruise*

Total Number of Copies   x $10.95 = _____

Plus shipping $2.00   _____

Plus sales tax (NJ only)   x $ .77 = _____

Total enclosed   _____

Name_____

Address_____

City _____ State _____ Zip _____

Ship to, if different:

Name_____

Address_____

City _____ State _____ Zip _____